AMERICAN ESTHER

Esther 4:14 "For such a time as this."

D A N I E L   R U B A L C A B A

WESTBOW
PRESS®
A DIVISION OF THOMAS NELSON
& ZONDERVAN

WestBow Press books may be ordered through booksellers or by contacting:

WestBow Press
A Division of Thomas Nelson & Zondervan
1663 Liberty Drive
Bloomington, IN 47403
www.westbowpress.com
844-714-3454

ISBN: 979-8-3850-2066-9 (sc)
ISBN: 979-8-3850-2067-6 (e)

Library of Congress Control Number: 2024904452

Print information available on the last page.

WestBow Press rev. date: 10/23/2024

CONTENTS

FORWARD

Esther was not one of the first books of the Bible I read after having been "born again" into the family of God. In fact, it was a couple of years before I took a reasonable look at Esther. Each time I've read it since, however, it's been a deepening pool of inspiration and revelation.

When I study Esther, it never lacks the reality nor the present power of God. When I finally became aware of the fact that God was not directly mentioned in the book, I was surprised and it wasn't because I had taken God for granted but instead, He never seemed absent from the text! The book never gave me any reason to question God's love and present concern for the people as I read. Although nothing has ever caused me to question God's love; the Book of Esther certainly did not.

Had I never known that God was not mentioned in this Esther, it wouldn't have detracted from its impact. I live in a world where our God is seldom mentioned in a positive or accurate way. Though this is tragic, it only serves to somehow enrich my personal relationship with The Lord, knowing how rare and priceless it really is.

In this increasingly apostate environment, wherein dwells all manner of atheistic, agnostic, and diabolical spirituality, God is going to accomplish a multifaceted work resulting in the greatest revival the world has ever seen, which will continue right through the greatest tribulation it has ever experienced. In the end, all will declare that "Jesus Christ is Lord!"

I am fully convinced that, given the opportunity, The Lord will miraculously express Himself to any generation of people. Obviously, we have God's Word; The Bible and we dare not tempt the absolute boundaries taught within it. Neither do we take for granted the rich and abundant written resources made available to us through hungry and determined hearts of super seekers who have gone before us. That being said, neither can we disregard the voice of God available through an intimate relationship with God having once submitted to the absolutes we referred to a moment ago.

For me, the continued unfurling of God's Word has been everything. I have always cried out to God for His immediate understanding, knowing that life is a vapor. From moment to moment, I have watched my precious Father God gently peel promises from divinely inspired pages and then adhere them onto my heart's most immediate need. To God be glory!

The following pages, I believe, will be a platform from which God will speak to you in a way that perhaps you have never before experienced, and I cannot over-emphasize its content.

ONE

The Flow

JUST AS GOD USED ESTHER TO RESCUE HIS PEOPLE, A DYNAMIC *flow of God's rescue will pour forth into every part of our nation. The focus of our study will be on one glorious aspect of that divine flow. This vessel, from which that glorious dynamic will flow, shall be a God-blessed and God-ordained contingency of women. Therefore, I will refer to them often and apply to them the truth of Esther. Notwithstanding, there are also shining examples of courage and integrity for every man who earnestly desires to be a witness for Christ in these last days. Mordecai exemplifies this powerfully.*

I pray your heart be open to the Word of God and surrender to its absolute authority. In doing so, you, too, can become a member of the Lord's corps of godly women, which will help steer this destruction-bound vessel onto a lifesaving course of revival and restoration!

> *Now these are the children of the province that went up out of the captivity, of those which had been carried away, whom Nebuchadnezzar the king of Babylon had carried away unto Babylon, and came*

again unto Jerusalem and Judah, every one unto his city (Ezra 2:1 KJV)

Contention

In the book of Ezra, a list is given of people who returned to Jerusalem and Judah at the end of the captivity. It is here that we find a point of contention among God's people for although many returned to the Promised Land, others chose to stay, having made Babylon their home. It is observed that when the account of the book of Esther was ultimately recorded, in protest of those Jews who chose to remain in Babylon, no mention of God was given in the account. Thus, we see that although all were Israelites, not all were fervently committed to their faith. To those who were, however, the thought of remaining in Babylon was inconceivable. Others couldn't or simply wouldn't leave.

Today, the people of America are very much the same. There are those who are fervently committed to her biblical foundations while others are not. Here also we are experiencing a strong contention between those who are holding to our biblical foundations while others choose a Babylonian lifestyle far removed from what is biblical.

TWO

The LORD is righteous; for I have rebelled against his commandment: hear, I pray you, all people, and behold my sorrow: my virgins and my young men are gone into captivity.
—Lamentations 1:18 (KJV)

For thus saith the LORD, That after seventy years be accomplished at Babylon I will visit you, and perform my good word toward you, in causing you to return to this place.
—Jeremiah 29:10 (KJV)

Captivity

ISRAEL HAD BEEN HELD CAPTIVE IN BABYLON FOR SEVENTY YEARS. *Simply stated, God's people brought upon themselves the painful defeats and sufferings as a result of disobeying the laws of God, primarily (but not limited to) those relating to the worship of idol gods. Generations before the actual captivity, the children of Israel had begun a gradual "turning away" from God. Eventually, they had wholly forsaken the laws of God and all that His covenant required. The people had developed a practice of making and worshipping idol gods. These were sins clearly defined and condemned in the first two of the Ten Commandments of God. Nevertheless, these dark devotions grew and ultimately became heinous forms of worship culminating in the sacrifice of children, and before it ended, thousands of children had*

3

been murdered. It was this disturbing and monstrous demonic practice that brought the judgment of God in the form of disgraceful defeat and captivity.

Listen to the Heart of God

> *Moreover the word of the LORD came unto me, saying,*
>
> *Now, thou son of man, wilt thou judge, wilt thou judge the bloody city? yea, thou shalt shew her all her abominations.*
>
> *Then say thou, Thus saith the Lord GOD, The city sheddeth blood in the midst of it, that her time may come, and maketh idols against herself to defile herself.*
>
> *(Ezekiel 22:1–3 KJV)*

Our purpose is to draw national parallels between historic Israel and our great nation, the United States of America. Now, the question is can we relate to this scenario in America, and if so, will it provide the answers you, the reader, need in order to be prepared for our future? I believe this volume will provide the lifesaving answers we desperately need.

It was at the end of this painful captivity when the amazing story of Esther took place.

THREE

Now it came to pass in the days of Ahasuerus, (this is Ahasuerus which reigned, from India even unto Ethiopia, over an hundred and seven and twenty provinces:).
—Esther 1:1–8 (KJV)

"In My Days"

IN ESTHER 1:1–8, WE SEE AN INCREDIBLE STORY BEING FRAMED *"in the days of Ahasuerus." In a moment we will discuss those days, but before we do, let us personalize the story for effectiveness by changing the words "in the days" to "in my days." All of the sudden, our perspective changes. We know that the power, riches, lands, security, and fame described in the first few verses are basically the pursuits of people today. Obviously, stuff has changed but not the general heart of the people; that really hasn't.*

What does change are the individual people from generation to generation; each of them being priceless and unique but given only a tiny space of time in the world. The Bible teaches us that our eternity will be experienced as a direct result to how we live our lives here.

Well then, if I asked you to describe "in my days" (your life and your world now), you would probably look around and then begin telling me what that looks like. And because I live in the same world you live in; we would agree on most things described.

This story is about a lot of things, conditions, situations, and people, but the most important part of it is you. This story is meant to inform, inspire, and challenge you. The Lord wants it to be all about you ... and Him. "Your days" are important to God, all that He has destined them to be—that is, greater than you ever imagined.

Ahasuerus

In the opening verses of Esther, we are immediately introduced to King Ahasuerus, whose throne is well established and secure, then we are given an overview of his vast kingdom along with its splendor and wealth. We are told it was the third year of his reign when he made a magnificent feast for his leaders, officials, and military officers while displaying before them the splendor and enormous wealth of his kingdom, and he did so for 180 days. It is interesting to consider the fact that just prior to this great feast, the king had convened a council to plan the invasion of Greece. The pomp and pride-filled exposé of this great feast isn't something we are not familiar with in our modern world; we see it all the time. In fact, it is a strong motivation for multitudes. Neither are we surprised when we learn of the planned invasion of Greece. Now, military aggression is in the news nearly every day.

Secrets Revealed

> *Then the king of Syria warred against Israel, and took counsel with his servants, saying, In such and such a place shall be my camp.*
>
> *And the man of God sent unto the king of Israel, saying, Beware that thou pass not such a place; for thither the Syrians are come down.*

And the king of Israel sent to the place which the man of God told him and warned him of, and saved himself there, not once nor twice.

Therefore the heart of the king of Syria was sore troubled for this thing; and he called his servants, and said unto them, Will ye not shew me which of us is for the king of Israel?

And one of his servants said, None, my lord, O king: but Elisha, the prophet that is in Israel, telleth the king of Israel the words that thou speakest in thy bedchamber.

(2 Kings 6:8–12 KJV)

Although the text does not mention the secret plans of King Ahasuerus to invade Greece, it is a historic fact. It is part of the existing environment during the story of Esther and is evidence of a large, multinational power struggle. To know much of what is unknown is part of God's equipping through the power of His Holy Spirit. It is made available specifically for God's children, primarily for evangelism along with the challenges that will inevitably come along the way. It is also given in order to warn the people (whomever that might be) of God's impending judgment.

In the scriptures above we see this awesome God-given ability functioning perfectly in the life and ministry of the prophet Elisha. Here, the secret military plans of the king of Syria are being thwarted simply by God telling Elisha what they are. The account states that the king of Israel was spared defeat more than once through this divine gift of revealing the enemies' plans.

Misused not Diffused

Much of what we have heard of as being the "prophetic gifting of God" has been exposed as being false simply through the passing of time. *The thing prophesied didn't happen. Perhaps they were right 50 percent of the time; does that qualify? Or perhaps the prophecy was vague and could ultimately be construed as being correct; does that qualify? No, neither one does; remember God is neither inconsistent nor is He vague, and He is never partially correct. Prophetic inconsistency does not necessarily disqualify one as being a Christian either. My purpose is not to be critical; however, prophetic accuracy will be one of the defining characteristics of leadership among God's remnant in these culminating days of history. True prophecy does not misrepresent God because it cannot violate biblical truth, and as a result it does not lack the dynamic force to move the people one way or another.*

A Secret Thing

It is easy to become so involved with our everyday lives that we lose that ever-growing and developing relationship with Christ and with His eternal kingdom. Although it is a Spiritual Kingdom, it is no less real than the temporal world, we live in. What God is doing there, is in direct relation to what He is doing here and because we are called to represent The Lord here, it is imperative that we are prophetically informed of approaching events, so that we can be prepared for them. This includes, to some degree, what our enemy the devil and his human cohorts are planning right now. We need to know the "who and how". I believe the Lord has provided that for us.

ALERT! There is a secret thing happening now, the details of which, I will reveal as we continue. Notwithstanding, there is infinite victory and peace in Christ Jesus for those who have determined to serve Him in these "last and perilous days". We will continually rejoice in that fact as we go.

FOUR

Esther 1:2-9 (KJV)

² That in those days, when the king Ahasuerus sat on the throne of his kingdom, which was in Shushan the palace,

³ In the third year of his reign, he made a feast unto all his princes and his servants; the power of Persia and Media, the nobles and princes of the provinces, being before him:

⁴ When he shewed the riches of his glorious kingdom and the honour of his excellent majesty many days, even an hundred and fourscore days.

⁵ And when these days were expired, the king made a feast unto all the people that were present in Shushan the palace, both unto great and small, seven days, in the court of the garden of the king's palace;

⁶ Where were white, green, and blue, hangings, fastened with cords of fine linen and purple to silver rings and pillars of marble: the beds were of gold and silver, upon a pavement of red, and blue, and white, and black, marble.

⁷ And they gave them drink in vessels of gold, (the vessels being diverse one from another,) and royal wine in abundance, according to the state of the king.

⁸ And the drinking was according to the law; none did compel: for so the king had appointed to all the officers of his house, that they should do according to every man's pleasure.

⁹ Also Vashti the queen made a feast for the women in the royal house which belonged to king Ahasuerus.

Cultural Shifting

Ahasuerus glories with pomp and splendor while confident in the strength and solidity of his throne. Then the celebration is moved to an even larger venue where more people can attend, those being the officials of a less formal nature and those higher levels of the general population.

It appears; some effort has been made to recognize the unique value of those who were in attendance, for each was given a golden vessel and no two were alike. Does this indicate that Ahasuerus was a 'people loving' person and genuinely concerned for the welfare of the individual? History seems to disprove the possibility.

Isn't it true that during election seasons, politicians go to great lengths to prove that they are deeply concerned for the individual? Yet when offices have been filled and a period passed, the phrase "one at a time" no longer applies. Unless, of course, another political battle needs to be won; then the individual will become important again.

Today we are experiencing a whole new reality, our political realm is steeped with spiritual significance. It is permeated by the spirit of anti-Christ. It has become a battleground for the soul of America.

For clarity, let us look at the folks who populate our government from a Biblical perspective. There are atheists who declare that there is no God. There are the religious who serve other gods not of the Bible (among whom are radical and open opponents of the American Republic). There are apostates who once served the true and living God of the Bible and have since forsaken it and now oppose it. There are hypocrites who say they serve the God of the Bible; however, their lifestyles are contrary to what the Bible teaches; and finally, there are genuine Children of God who whole-heartedly serve God according to the Bible in all circumstances.

Biblical teaching (which is the very foundation of our nation and republic) always directs us to appreciate every individual person as a priceless soul for whom Jesus died on the cross of Calvary and to minister both spiritually and practically to each need. This, in a nutshell, describes a healthy Bible based society. It will ultimately be described as a righteous nation based upon Biblical truth.

Now, however, we are seeing more and more the recognition and appreciation of the individual embraced by current politicians and elected officials who at the same time, whole-heartedly reject the Bible along with its teaching, and those who faithfully serve and promote the God of The Bible. These are they who go so far as to criminalize the Word of God.

Their declarations sound good and their motives seem pure; they are, however, counterfeit and designed to mimic the goodness of God to persuade the people that they themselves are good, and that Christians are evil. This is the spirit of anti-Christ. The ultimate goal is to remove the Christian influence from society. The reason? It is because this holy influence is the only power on earth that can thwart their anti-Bible agenda.

FIVE

<u>Culture Shifting</u>

<u>1. "Have it your way"</u>

Ahasuerus provides that the booze will flow freely for as long as the celebrations last, with one stipulation, there is a law which states that the people are not to be compelled regarding their drinking. The law states that you may drink as little or as much as you please. In other words, the law must be relaxed; "have it your way" … pleasure is the law of the day.

<u>Pleasure?</u>

> *Hebrews 11:24-25 (KJV)*
> *[24] By faith Moses, when he was come to years, refused to be called the son of Pharaoh's daughter;*
> *[25] Choosing rather to suffer affliction with the people of God, than to enjoy the pleasures of sin for a season;*

From The New Testament retrospect, Egypt is a type; it typifies the lifestyle of one who is lost in sins. It refers to the life that is lived routinely practicing the sorts of actions which the Bible defines as sin and eventually leads to slavery or addiction to them. They are done purely for the satisfaction of the fleshly lusts and sinful pleasures.

There is a plethora of activities whether done alone or with others which fall under the heading of sin. These same practices were available to Moses while he remained in Egypt, however, once he learned of His true identity, revolted against its unrighteous practices and was quickly deemed a criminal (which is the criminalization of righteousness). The liberty to exercise his every lustful whim was unlimited as a prince of Egypt yet none of that was reason to remain. The idolatrous sin of Egypt only enslaved the people, crushing the innocent. Moses, in his flight, would discover God's better way.

> *Romans 1:29-32 (KJV)*
> *29 Being filled with all unrighteousness, fornication, wickedness, covetousness, maliciousness; full of envy, murder, debate, deceit, malignity; whisperers,*
> *30 Backbiters, haters of God, despiteful, proud, boasters, inventors of evil things, disobedient to parents,*
> *31 Without understanding, covenant breakers, without natural affection, implacable, unmerciful:*
> *32 Who knowing the judgment of God, that they which commit such things are worthy of death, not only do the same, but have pleasure in them that do them.*

What a list, the Apostle Paul lays out for us. It reeks of rotting and malignity, and yet, seems to describe the moral condition of our country and world today.

It is an intense description of the actions and attitudes of a population whose pursuit in life is of physical pleasure; then shockingly goes on to display a people who know better, being familiar with the Laws and judgements of God, but instead of strongly correcting them are more concerned with pleasing them.

As a result, laws prohibiting these things are changed in order to facilitate them. Vile pleasures become the law of the land while the "haters of God" (Romans 1:30) prosecute these new laws in hopes of dismantling God's people.

In this cultural shift, Christians are characterized as the oppressors of the people.

Jesus said," ¹⁸ If the world hate you, ye know that it hated me before it <u>hated</u> you." John 15:18 (KJV) The word is hated (detested), and it describes as to what degree Christians are already hated in the womb of this cultural shift. Allowed to continue, this hatred will grow in expression against the Church beginning with mild opposition and progressing into outright violence. This is the dark plan of an eternally blackened heart and the dark secret I referred to earlier.

> *Isaiah 5:20 (ASV)*
> *²⁰ Woe unto them that call <u>evil good, and good evil; that put darkness for light, and light for darkness; that put bitter for sweet, and sweet for bitter!</u>*

(Isaiah 5:20, perfectly describes what this anti-Christ agenda is!)

Unequivocally stated, what fuels this cultural effort is hatred toward God, His Son Jesus Christ, The Holy Bible, and God's Holy Remnant- His people.

SIX

Esther 1:9-17 (ASV)

⁹ *Also Vashti the queen made a feast for the women in the royal house which belonged to king Ahasuerus.*

¹⁰ *On the seventh day, when the heart of the king was merry with wine, he commanded Mehuman, Biztha, Harbona, Bigtha, and Abagtha, Zethar, and Carcas, the seven chamberlains that ministered in the presence of Ahasuerus the king,*

¹¹ *to bring Vashti the queen before the king with the crown royal, to show the peoples and the princes her beauty; for she was fair to look on.*

¹² *But the queen Vashti refused to come at the king's commandment by the chamberlains: therefore was the king very wroth, and his anger burned in him.*

¹³ *Then the king said to the wise men, who knew the times, (for so was the king's manner toward all that knew law and judgment;*

¹⁴ *and the next unto him were Carshena, Shethar, Admatha, Tarshish, Meres, Marsena, and Memucan, the seven princes of Persia and*

Media, who saw the king's face, and sat first in the kingdom),

¹⁵ What shall we do unto the queen Vashti according to law, because she hath not done the bidding of the king Ahasuerus by the chamberlains?

¹⁶ And Memucan answered before the king and the princes, Vashti the queen hath not done wrong to the king only, but also to all the princes, and to all the peoples that are in all the provinces of the king Ahasuerus.

¹⁷ For this deed of the queen will come abroad unto all women, to make their husbands contemptible in their eyes, when it shall be reported, The king Ahasuerus commanded Vashti the queen to be brought in before him, but she came not.

Feasting

In verse 9 we see that two separate feasts are happening simultaneously. The king's feast, which was for men only and Vashti his wife's feast which was exclusively for the women. It seems as though Vashti is only a footnote to the story, however, a request by the king places Vashti at the very epicenter of the story. If it had not been for the king's request, we may not have ever known Vashti.

Perhaps it's more important, at this point, to focus upon the king's drunken state. It is in the alcoholic drunken state where normal inhibitions are lifted. The king orders that Vashti should be summoned to leave her feast and immediately come to the king's. The purpose, that he might display her beauty before all the men who were present with him. Some suggest that perhaps her nudity was being ordered, others disagree saying established Persian laws and customs guarding women and keeping them separate from *men were being violated. This, in their estimation, was sufficient dishonoring of Vashti and would justify her action. Still others disagree. Either way, a notable resistance is revealed in Vashti.*

The Weakened King

To what the king envisioned her doing that day, Vashti refused. Was her bold refusal a sign of her strength? Was it a sign of the king's weakness? I am convinced it was both. It is probable that no one knew the king better than his wife. Could she have known what his reaction to her refusal would be?

The account says that the king was wroth and that his anger burned in him, yet she was not physically disciplined nor was she imprisoned, in fact, there is no mention of the king immediately confronting her at all.

Cultural Shifting

2. Masculine Integrity Lost

> *1 Peter 3:7 (KJV)*
> *⁷ Likewise, ye husbands, dwell with them according to knowledge, giving honour unto the wife, as unto the weaker vessel, and as being heirs together of the grace of life; that your prayers be not hindered.*

Let me remind you that our avenue of description is a Spiritually prophetic one. It is a revealing of secret warfare, its planning, and how those plans are unfolding in our country today. The plan of our enemy is for you to see that what is culturally happening now, is purely the process of growth and human development and that it is the work of adequate and caring men and women and that, it has nothing to do with the Bible. This is absolutely wrong; this has everything to do with the Bible and there is so much more that you must see. Let us continue.

When the flow of God's program is interrupted, problems begin to develop within the family. Left unchecked this family disruption becomes a social disruption and eventually a cultural shift. Because it began contrary to God's will for the family; each shift which occurs as a result is also wrong, being contrary to what God has ordained. Eventually it will fall. It is this fall we want to prevent, however, if we cannot prevent its collapse, then we must work diligently to harvest as many precious souls as possible prior to its fall. For either conclusion to take place, we must be prophetically informed.

Husbands!

The Apostle Peter instructs that we husbands must dwell with our wives according to knowledge. Obviously in marriage there is no end to learning; this refers to many lessons, however, the foundational knowledge referred to is what is taught in the Bible.

The word <u>dwell</u> means to live together as a family and that being according to Bible knowledge or what God has commanded. As you know, these truths, meet with determined and even heated opposition today. This type of opposition, however, does not surprise us. Today's generation of Christians are being confronted by an evil mandate, which the Bible foresaw centuries ago. Nevertheless, the truth of God's Word must be declared even as it relates to marriage.

It is stated that the husband must honor his wife as the weaker vessel. This is not saying inferior but weaker. In our day, we celebrate differences and yet when one of our differences is distinguished as being physically weaker, it is rejected. It is, nonetheless, a matter of fact. So, the most basic concern for a good husband is to shore up, in his wife, physical weakness in comparison to the strength of any man. This is simply what the Persian custom had established. Biblically, there is much more taught, yet this very basic protection is also required.

Another facet is the issue of authority. In today's female population, the virtue of male protection is only slightly questioned, however, when the concept of male authority over women is asserted, sparks begin to fly. Remember, just because Biblical Truth is rejected, does not make it old fashioned nor outdated. In fact, it is the very re-establishing of God's Authority that we are fearfully praying and preparing for! (It's ultimate re-establishing will shake our land!)

Vashti ignored both the power and authority of King Ahasuerus, who was one of the most powerful kings on earth. Simply stated (and absolutely true both then and now), when in marriage, the integrity of masculinity declines, the integrity of femininity also declines. It does not stop there either. It spills over into every facet of society until even the most basic truths of human life, existence, function, and associations are questioned more and more frequently. It is at this point, that God will delude a society of people. Why? Because as this condition progresses, the most innocent of society will be misdirected, neglected, and finally rejected (abortion).

What does delusion do? It is God giving up on a people who refuse to turn-around. It causes them to believe their own lies. Feeling justified in all their evil actions, they steam-roll ahead! In other words, it actually hastens or expedites the process of judgment in order to spare the innocent and for the Glory of His Name.

This my children, is why we so desperately want to understand our culture and at what point prophetically we are! As the trumpet sounds our dispatch, we must know how to respond!

SEVEN

<u>Culture Shifting</u>
<u>3. The Decline of Biblical Femininity</u>

<u>The Danger of Radical Feminism</u>

Esther 1:13,15,17–18 (KJV)
[13] Then the king said to the wise men, which knew the times, (for so was the king's manner toward all that knew law and judgment:

[15] What shall we do unto the queen Vashti according to law, because she hath not performed the commandment of the king Ahasuerus by the chamberlains?

[17] For this deed of the queen shall come abroad unto all women, so that they shall despise their husbands in their eyes, when it shall be reported, The king Ahasuerus commanded Vashti the queen to be brought in before him, but she came not.

[18] Likewise shall the ladies of Persia and Media say this day unto all the king's princes, which have heard of the deed of the queen. Thus shall there arise too much contempt and wrath.

What Shall We Do?

Time has passed. Emotions have subsided. Finally, the king seeks guidance from those wise and learned men of the law and judgment. What shall we do?

Before we proceed, it is important that we do not diminish the importance of what the king Ahasuerus is doing. He has gathered people who will help to make the best decision possible as it relates to Vashti's refusal to obey the kings request. Probably, after having recovered from his drunken state, he has realized the volatile circumstance that has risen out of his decision to call Vashti over to his feast.

It is not our purpose to justify or vilify the actions of the individuals involved, but rather to realize the danger that is evident to them should Vashti's action spark an uprising of women against their husbands. The statement would seem funny if it wasn't so relevant. It isn't a joke; it is a plan. A plan to undermine the very social fabric of our Biblically based society.

Esther 1:18 (KJV) [18] Likewise shall the ladies of Persia and Media say this day unto all the king's princes, which have heard of the deed of the queen. Thus shall there arise too much contempt and wrath.

It is a condition that is deeply rooted within our embattled society already. It is far reaching and incredibly dangerous, having morphed into a deadly killing machine devouring millions of our most vulnerable and innocent. Indeed, there has risen too much contempt and wrath!

Danger to Danger

This new cultural shift brings danger on three levels. First, the proven ongoing danger it brings to our current child population from conception to adulthood, and yes, we have staggering statistics to prove it.

The second danger, which is now beginning to manifest, is the vilifying of True Christianity, those who adhere to the "whole council of God" (The entire Bible cover to cover). These are they who represent Christ in flesh (The Body of Christ) and strike fear in the heart of Satan.

The third and most ominous of all, is the increasing discontentment in the Heart of God for what He is witnessing and experiencing Himself. His massive discontentment will eventually break forth upon the perpetrators of this present evil!

It is the combination of diminishing male masculinity and the uprising of unhealthy feminine authority from which we are seeing emerge a radical and dangerous environment and let me remind you that our point of reference is the Holy Bible, the Word of God; for which we make no apologies. To deny or ignore the increasingly toxic nature of our society would be tragic. Furthermore, these things are not incidental, they are of a precise and dastardly design and even though we have seen them develop in the past these will continue to develop until the end! Are you ready?

> *Esther 1:19-20 (KJV)*
> *¹⁹ If it please the king, let there go a royal commandment from him, and let it be written among the laws of the Persians and the Medes, that it be not altered, That Vashti come no more before king Ahasuerus; and let the king give her royal estate unto another that is better than she.*
> *²⁰ And when the king's decree which he shall make shall be published throughout all his empire, (for it is great,) all the wives shall give to their husbands honour, both to great and small.*

Decree

It is agreed that once the king's decree is announced that it will safeguard the continued family structure wherein the husband is the chief authority and protector of wife and children.

Once again, it is not our purpose to establish virtue among these men; they were not good people, however, it is imperative that we recognize, at least, their understanding of a certain family structure and how without it, the society as a whole, would ultimately become impossible to govern.

Reality Overview

Should we diagnose our current social condition based upon what we have gleaned thus far, we would agree that the same components exist, only more advanced and alarming!

1. *The legalization of all forms of pleasure*
2. *The minimization of (Biblical) masculine integrity of husbands*
3. *The minimization of (Biblical) feminine integrity of wives*
4. *The minimization of the healthy nuclear family with husband as its head*
5. *The rise of an unhealthy even radical feminism*
6. *The hidden plans and influences associated with the constant threat of war*

God's Hidden Plan Revealed

> *Esther 2:4–8 (KJV)*
> *⁴ And let the maiden which pleaseth the king be queen instead of Vashti. And the thing pleased the king; and he did so.*

⁵ Now in Shushan the palace there was a certain Jew, whose name was Mordecai, the son of Jair, the son of Shimei, the son of Kish, a Benjamite;

⁶ Who had been carried away from Jerusalem with the captivity which had been carried away with Jeconiah king of Judah, whom Nebuchadnezzar the king of Babylon had carried away.

⁷ And he brought up Hadassah, that is, Esther, his uncle's daughter: for she had neither father nor mother, and the maid was fair and beautiful; whom Mordecai, when her father and mother were dead, took for his own daughter.

⁸ So it came to pass, when the king's commandment and his decree was heard, and when many maidens were gathered together unto Shushan the palace, to the custody of Hegai, that Esther was brought also unto the king's house, to the custody of Hegai, keeper of the women.

Esther 2:1-2 (KJV)

¹ After these things, when the wrath of king Ahasuerus was appeased, he remembered Vashti, and what she had done, and what was decreed against her.

² Then said the king's servants that ministered unto him, Let there be fair young virgins sought for the king:

Esther 2:4 (KJV)

⁴ And let the maiden which pleaseth the king be queen instead of Vashti. And the thing pleased the king; and he did so.

Esther 2:16-17 (KJV)

¹⁶ So Esther was taken unto king Ahasuerus into his house royal in the tenth month, which is the month Tebeth, in the seventh year of his reign.

¹⁷ And the king loved Esther above all the women, and she obtained grace and favour in his sight more than all the virgins; so that he set the royal crown upon her head, and made her queen instead of Vashti.

The Search for One Better Than Vashti

There is no way to over-emphasize the danger that was lurking around the corner and the desolation it would leave in its wake. Only God knew the cloud of murderous intent which was about to rain upon God's people, and He alone could deliver them. It now hinges upon the selection made for Vashti's replacement.

It is no exaggeration to say that we in America are facing the same level of danger, in fact, the groundwork is already completed and if successfully executed, it would be a massive defeat and overthrow!

In this Biblical and historic account, the vulnerability the Jews are exposed to, is due to their own rebellion against God's authority; they constantly ignored His laws and the prophetic warnings which ensued. Therefore, the captivity, was their fault not God's.

(Galatians 6:7 (KJV) ⁷ Be not deceived; God is not mocked: for whatsoever a man soweth, that shall he also reap.) Thus, we too, have unknowingly sown seeds of rebellion which have grown up into the most organized and determined assault against God's people ever, here in the United States.

"You seem to warn exclusively the U.S. but doesn't this apply to the whole world," you ask? I speak exclusively of the U.S. for

25

two reasons. First, I am called as a voice to this nation, my country. Secondly, the U.S. is unique because of her foundations. She was founded as a Christian nation and built up according to Biblical truth. In essence, the U.S.A has covenant with God which makes her immensely unique among all the gentile nations of the earth!)

In other words, we have created our own vulnerability and deficit of power by assault upon our children including abortion, removal of prayer and Bible study from schools, most fundamentally, the learning of the Ten Commandments.

This same wicked authority which has freely crushed the innocent is about to launch the most devious and murderous plan that our world has ever seen or felt. Our deliverance again hinges upon a selection that God is making even now, just as He did in the time of Esther!

It is a dual mandate we face. First, we must make a conscious and calculated move of repentance toward God All Mighty. Secondly, we must free ourselves from the thick and heavy deception which is being thrust upon our whole society at an unprecedented rate. We need clear witness from God, a miraculous awakening, and deliverance.

Divinely Predestined

Esther 2:5-6 (KJV)
5 Now in Shushan the palace there was a certain Jew, whose name was Mordecai, the son of Jair, the son of Shimei, the son of Kish, a Benjamite;
6 Who had been carried away from Jerusalem with the captivity which had been carried away with Jeconiah king of Judah, whom Nebuchadnezzar the king of Babylon had carried away.

Ezra 2:1-2 (KJV)

¹ Now these are the children of the province that went up out of the captivity, of those which had been carried away, whom Nebuchadnezzar the king of Babylon had carried away unto Babylon, and came again unto Jerusalem and Judah, every one unto his city;

² Which came with Zerubbabel: Jeshua, Nehemiah, Seraiah, Reelaiah, <u>Mordecai</u>, Bilshan, Mispar, Bigvai, Rehum, Baanah. The number of the men of the people of Israel:

Here in Esther 2:5, we are introduced to Mordecai and in Ezra 2:1-2, Mordecai is mentioned as one of the first to return to Jerusalem, helping in the early stages of resettling of the people, then returned to Persia while the temple construction was stalled. Mordecai is not just another Jew but a leader among them. It appears he has already been involved in the rebuilding of Jerusalem.

<u>*And he brought up Hadassah, that is, Esther*</u>

Esther 2:7 (KJV)

⁷ And he brought up Hadassah, that is, Esther, his uncle's daughter: for she had neither father nor mother, and the maid was fair and beautiful; whom Mordecai, when her father and mother were dead, took for his own daughter.

Isn't it interesting that when we are introduced to Esther she is called 'Hadassah'? Hadassah refers to the feminine part of 'love and marriage'. Family is God's structure given for the peace and perpetuation of all humanity. It is also the vivid illustration of God's love for his people.

It is at this juncture that we begin to see a huge part of God's plan for the rescue of America as a nation, who unknowingly are standing upon the strong foundation of God's Word, The Bible.

In my last book "Blind Faith" we spelled out The Lord's call for the restoration of a great army of Godly men. Here we are seeing the plan of God for the fresh unveiling of the second facet of that great army, Godly women, co-champions of the Biblical Family. She will display the type of beauty, grace and courage that will be impossible for God to resist. What a beautiful description of the ones whom God has chosen to replace a Vashti movement.

The Choice

I whole heartedly believe that the "prince of the darkness of this world" has launched his last great assault upon the Kingdom of God here on earth. He assails to destroy both the Church and Israel. He is feverously working to intoxicate whole nations of people including the United States in order to eventually vilify both Christians and Jews. His ultimate goal, to turn hate into violence and then direct it upon God's people. It is impossible to imagine the violence which is about to break forth against all that is Good.

What is God doing in response to this evil thrust? He is intentionally and quietly making a choice. He is choosing one by one and raising up a glorious army of Godly women, indeed, an army of intercessors, the likes of which, the world has never seen.

Lady, you mustn't take this divine choosing for granted. There is too much at stake. This is your calling, your destiny, your purpose! Your time has come!

> *Esther 2:8-9 (KJV)*
> *⁸ So it came to pass, when the king's commandment and his decree was heard, and when many maidens were gathered together unto Shushan the palace, to the custody of Hegai, that Esther was brought*

also unto the king's house, to the custody of Hegai, keeper of the women.

And he preferred her and her maids unto the best place of the house of the women.

A Eunuch's Response

Let's compare this preparation and selection process with our current social perspective and priorities. From today's carnal and sensual estimation, this selection would begin outwardly and would represent eighty percent of the overall reason for selection, a beauty pageant if you would. Eventually the inward virtues or lack thereof would be noted. In other words, the criterion for choosing a maiden would reflect the heart and integrity of the individual making the choice.

In Hegai, the eunuch, the keeper of the women, there are none of the sensual influences present in his response toward Esther as would be in our society and certainly would have been in King Ahasuerus. Hegai would become familiar with the heart of Esther and was deeply moved when he discovered it.

Jesus didn't say that we would know a person by their outward appearance but rather by their fruits or works. Samuel also, when told by God to select a king among Jessie's sons, was given wisdom of God when the Lord instructed him not to look upon the outward man but instead to await God's selection. He, sees within the heart.

This is what the Lord is doing now! He is looking within. Simply stated, God is making the choice and although people are involved, it is God's hand which is touching and preparing these special ladies to bring powerful deliverance into the world.

Hegai was also a man of authority and trusted by leadership. He recognized the majesty of a good and true leader and he perceived it early in Esther. Seeing virtue in Esther and great benefit to the nation, Hegai moved quickly, providing her with every possible *advantage and support in preparation for her meeting with the king.*

This is God's favor! Once the choosing of an individual is made, The Holy Ghost will immediately begin to provide each lady with all the necessary anointings and giftings necessary for the effective completion of the divine task. Awesome! This will be an exciting time in American History!

Overwhelmed?

"I don't doubt the glorious plan of God," you say, "However, is it even possible for me to be a soldier in this last day army?"

Not only is it possible, but necessary, besides, you've had a fire burning in your heart for a while now. You've longed for God's intervention! You can hardly bear the pain and destruction along with the hate and injustice. You've wept before the Lord many times and it isn't as though you haven't served the Lord in the past, however, now ... it breaks your heart and at times consumes you. "Please Lord!", you cry. You know what the Bible says about the "last days" including the dire and difficult circumstances that will exist! Still, you long to be involved! Not moved by fear; you are moved by conviction and you only want to make a difference.

If what I have said bears witness in your heart, I say, "Welcome to this great calling and effort". Jesus spoke of wars and rumors of wars when describing the "last days" and indeed we are seeing nations preparing more and more for conflict. I am convinced, however, that the greatest war ever fought for our nation will be a spiritual one!

Jeremiah 29:11 (KJV)
[11] For I know the thoughts that I think toward you, saith the LORD, thoughts of peace, and not of evil, to give you an expected end.

More than Fate

It is easy to feel frustrated and insignificant when you are daily confronted with the darkness that is descending upon our people. Our faith ebbs and flows according to our emotions and then we end up appraising our worth according to successes. We are constantly comparing ourselves with others especially with endless social media which only distorts the plan and process of God. This great battle will not be fought before the multitudes. Neither will His recruiting be done this way, in fact, it will be done in secret places of prayer. The one thing you need is what the "web" cannot produce ... quiet time alone with God.

God will use you in an awesome way, not because He happened upon you. No, there is more; He is there because you were destined to be exactly who you are now, the lady he has created you to be! He loves you and is drawn to you in this critical hour. All this was planned and accomplished through the shed blood of Jesus.

Rejoice! You are not an accident nor are you Plan B! You are It! Along with many others who will move the Hand of God to do marvelous wonders in this great nation and world.

EIGHT

Qualified

Romans 8:14-16 (KJV)
14 For as many as are led by the Spirit of God, they are the sons of God.
15 For ye have not received the spirit of bondage again to fear; but ye have received the Spirit of adoption, whereby we cry, Abba, Father.
16 The Spirit itself beareth witness with our spirit, that we are the children of God:

Galatians 4:6-7 (KJV)
6 And because ye are sons, God hath sent forth the Spirit of his Son into your hearts, crying, Abba, Father.
7 Wherefore thou art no more a servant, but a son; and if a son, then an heir of God through Christ.

We were told in Esther 2:2 that Mordecai had adopted Esther, her having neither father nor mother. The Glorious truth is that while God's people were approaching a desperate need for a miracle, the adoption of Esther had placed her where she needed to be in order for God to deliver that miracle!

There is so much to be gained from the study of Esther. The account abounds with the miraculous hand of God at work. The graceful even poetic weaving of God's purpose is amazing and inspires us to believe that we too can be included in His Plan. God had determined to deliver His people from an overwhelming threat and with His power, accomplished that goal! Today, He is doing it again. His plan is perfect; His choices are sound; His heart is set ... He will not fail!

It is my desire to encourage you to find your place in this great move of God's deliverance; do it now before it's too late. There is a place for you in His plan!

A critical step toward the salvation of God's people, has been taken: Mordecai's adoption of Esther! The importance of it cannot be over emphasized. What was a miracle to Esther alone will soon become a miracle to multitudes! It was Esther's adoption which qualified her for the amazing role she would play in God's plan to deliver His people.

Children not Servants

I remember attending church as a boy. I also attended the weekly school sessions. I did what I was told and learned what I was taught; I even practiced religion for a while mostly out of fear. I cannot remember ever being stirred in my heart or warmed spiritually by what was taking place in the service there and yet I felt it was somehow necessary. I always considered myself part of it even while I walked away and stayed away. Ultimately The Lord began to move in my heart, however, that church was not the place I considered returning to.

Many people attended there and still do. I had respect for it and honored those in charge, nevertheless, it could not have possibly qualified me for what I do now. Why? Because they told me I was a child of God, but I never felt as though I was. Nothing there convinced me that I was.

There was something else happening in my life during those

same years but not in a church. It was at school, a country school. We would pray and sing and occasionally read the Bible. It was there that I would feel the stirring of God's love in my six-year-old heart. I would become emotional! Perhaps it showed. Later, my teacher asked me if I would read a portion of Luke's gospel in the Christmas play. I remember reading the scripture that night as though it was last night. I never felt more special than that night. You see, the One who is my Creator was longing to be my Father! Hallelujah!

In Romans 8 and Ephesians 4 we are told that we are given, into our hearts, a Spirit of adoption and that it causes us to cry out calling God our Abba Father. Furthermore, it identifies that Spirit as the Spirit of His Son Jesus and that He declares that we are no longer servants but are Children and Sons of God! Hallelujah! This is Jesus Christ who whispers in your heart and tells you that you have miraculously become a Child of God.

It is this adoption which qualifies you to fulfill your role in this glorious move of God just as Esther's adoption qualified her.

Prayer to be Born Again (Saved and Adopted)

Dear God, I am a sinner in desperate need of a savior. The Bible says that Jesus Christ your son is the only true Savior.

Therefore, at His feet I kneel. Lord Jesus forgive my sins. Wash me with your blood. I surrender my life to you. I want to serve you. I receive you with joy as my Lord and Savior. I both need you and desire you in my life. I know that you love me. You proved that on the cross of Calvary. I turn from my sinful ways and commit myself to loving you in word and deed with all of my heart forever and forever. Now touch me, teach me, and take me wherever you choose that I may represent you faithfully and preach the Gospel powerfully. Amen

Pleasing

> ### Esther 2:9 (KJV)
> [9] And the maiden pleased him, and she obtained kindness of him; and he speedily gave her things for purification, with such things as belonged to her, and seven maidens, which were meet to be given her, out of the king's house: and he preferred her and her maids unto the best place of the house of the women.

> ### John 8:28-29 (KJV)
> [28] Then said Jesus unto them, When ye have lifted up the Son of man, then shall ye know that I am he, and that I do nothing of myself; but as my Father hath taught me, I speak these things.
> [29] And he that sent me is with me: the Father hath not left me alone; for I do always those things that please him. John [8]:[28]-[29] (KJV)

Above in v.28 Jesus reveals that His life has a plan and that it requires his self-less obedience. He continues by telling us that he has been taught and that He never deviates from those lessons. Furthermore, in v.29 He continues by telling us that He both speaks and does whatever His Father has taught Him. This is how He pleases His Father! Therefore, to be pleasing to God is as simple as learning His Word and always adhering to the lessons provided.

Esther pleased Hegai the keeper of the maidens. It was her character which pleased the eunuch above all else. We don't deny her physical beauty, however, Esther was far more than that. As you will see, she was a marvelous daughter to Mordecai. She was genuine in her exceptional obedience never considering it a burden. Mordecai was simply her father and *from all we can gather, she had become like him in spirit, heart, and mind.*

It was this core beauty which was foundational to her exterior beauty and not the other way around. It was irresistible to Hegai and he immediately began to favor her with all the advantages available to her including seven maiden servants. His favor for Esther was, in fact, so great that she and her maidens were given the best place in the house.

NINE

Esther 2:10-11 (KJV)
¹⁰ Esther had not shewed her people nor her kindred: for Mordecai had charged her that she should not shew it.

<u>*Veiled Identity*</u>

Esther had not revealed her people nor ethnicity because her father Mordecai had told her not to. Esther was not Persian but rather a Jew which would expose her to danger; this was Mordecai's concern. Both of her parents were dead and unknown to the Persians involved. They assumed she was Persian.

John 17:14 (KJV)
¹⁴ I have given them thy word; and the world hath hated them, because they are not of the world, even as I am not of the world.

Matthew 10:16 (KJV)
¹⁶ Behold, I send you forth as sheep in the midst of wolves: be ye therefore wise as serpents, and harmless as doves.

It's amazing that we too are given tasks in this world,

a world, that according to the words of Jesus; (John 17:14) " ...we are not of." Furthermore, the Lord characterizes the dangerous nature of our task when in (Matt. 10:16) he likens us to kingdom sheep sent forth into a world containing wolves who viciously and ferociously oppose our work.

No, it is not important that we continually declare our heavenly citizenship as long as we can fulfill our task of rescuing those for whom Jesus died. We must fulfill the Will of God relating to the children, the redeemed, and the elect. There is much work to be done. The name and DNA they need is of Jesus, not of us.

> John 14:1-3 (KJV)
> ¹ Let not your heart be troubled: ye believe in God, believe also in me.
> ² In my Father's house are many mansions: if it were not so, I would have told you. I go to prepare a place for you.
> ³ And if I go and prepare a place for you, I will come again, and receive you unto myself; that where I am, there ye may be also.

We know that Jesus began His earthly life as the infant child of Mary and Joseph. His physical growth and maturation were not unusual at least as far as we know. He grew and developed and, in the process, became aware of the people and world around him.

His growing awareness, however, was of more than just the physical world; He was becoming aware of eternal things, things spiritual in nature. He spoke of His Holy Father and His eternal kingdom. He spoke of it as his home, the place where He had come from and the place He would return to.

Earlier we heard Jesus as he prayed declare that we, like Him, *are not of this world. Through the Lord's teaching, He purposefully made us aware of an eternal kingdom and that it is the Christian's destination and ultimately home.*

He further declared that we are more than servants of that kingdom; we are children of it.

So how important is it that we know that we are children of that kingdom and that it is a foregone conclusion that we too will someday go there and abide forever?!

Very important! Why? Because as we press forward and labor in the field of our Father, we will know that we are representing more than ourselves. We are representing an eternal kingdom filled with those who have felt just as we do now! They were firebrands! They fought and have finished. (Heb. 12) Now as they behold, we too will fight and finish! Hallelujah!

¹¹ And Mordecai walked every day before the court of the women's house, to know how Esther did, <u>and what should become of her.</u>

The account shows us that Mordecai had daily walked where Esther lived for twelve months. He watched and prayed for Esther as her preparations to stand before King Ahasuerus continued.

When we have surrendered our lives, for whatever tasks the Lord will choose, we can be sure that they will have eternal significance, involving the rescuing of lives through salvation.

From beginning to end, the Lord will be with us and not just for the sake of observation. He is there with the heart of a loving Father, concerned for us as we minister His loving desire for the need of others. It is love which motivates Him! Can you imagine ... infinite God; immeasurable, all powerful, all mighty God and still concerned for us. Amazing! When Jesus said in Matthew 28:20

(KJV), "I am with you always, even unto the end of the world. Amen." He meant it! Hallelujah!

> Esther 2:12 (KJV)
> [12] Now when every maid's turn was come to go in to king Ahasuerus, after that she had been twelve months, according to the manner of the women, (for so were the days of their purifications accomplished, to wit, six months with oil of myrrh, and six months with sweet odours, and with other things for the purifying of the women;)

Esther's Time

Esther's turn before the king was approaching and she couldn't know the importance of it. It is in this area where we as God's people must become aware of what approaches. We are living in perilous times but what does that mean?

2 Timothy 3:12-13 (KJV) "12 Yea, and all that will live godly in Christ Jesus shall suffer persecution. 13 But evil men and seducers shall wax worse and worse, deceiving, and being deceived."

The word speaks clearly as to how difficult it will become for true Christians in the near future! For us to deny this would be unfruitful. For us to attempt to change their inevitability would be useless for they are already upon us.

What we can do, however, and what we must do is to allow God to position us into a place where we can be used in a life-saving way. We don't need to know the details of what that looks like either. As with Esther, being favored is the key, not knowing every detail of the future but instead being prepared for any future. God will anoint you and me with "myrr and sweet fragrances" to effectively *stand before any opposing man or devil. We will rise above them, and in the process rescue the souls of multitudes for God's Glory!*

The secular world boasts of a powerful women's movement unveiling, but forgive my English when I shout,"They ain't seen nothin yet!" To Christ be Glory! Hallelujah!

Purifying

The Word tells us that Esther received one year of purification, six months with the oil of myrrh and six months with sweet odours.

The combination of the two remedies provided for the entire body beginning with the skin and continuing inward for overall health. We cannot dispute the effectiveness of these oils and balsams etc., they are still being used today. Esther responded to these therapies as well as anyone of them. Esther's beauty was illuminated and made vibrant which would immediately appeal to Ahasuerus. He would see her as a glowing queen, a trophy by his side, and a vindication for his ousting of Vashti.

To God, however, it was her inward beauty which was compelling. Holy means; having spiritual health. It was within that beauty that He could see a deliverer of His people. Esther would be God's glory and for all times declare; that soft and subtle does not mean weak and unusable.

TEN

Spiritual Work

John 6:53-58 (KJV)
⁵³ Then Jesus said unto them, Verily, verily, I say unto you, Except ye eat the flesh of the Son of man, and drink his blood, ye have no life in you.

⁵⁴ Whoso eateth my flesh, and drinketh my blood, hath eternal life; and I will raise him up at the last day.

⁵⁵ For my flesh is meat indeed, and my blood is drink indeed.

⁵⁶ He that eateth my flesh, and drinketh my blood, dwelleth in me, and I in him.

⁵⁷ As the living Father hath sent me, and I live by the Father: so he that eateth me, even he shall live by me.

⁵⁸ This is that bread which came down from heaven: not as your fathers did eat manna, and are dead: he that eateth of this bread shall live forever.

John 6:63 (KJV)
⁶³ It is the spirit that quickeneth; the flesh profiteth nothing: the words that I speak unto you, they are spirit, and they are life.

Our work as God's people is always a spiritual endeavor. Let me show you why. Hundreds of people were following Jesus but after the Lord had spoken these words at least four hundred left. The Lord had informed them that unless they eat his body and drink his blood, they would not qualify to be his apostles. It sounded like cannibalism to them, something horrible at least.

The Lord knew they would respond this way, most of us would have also. The Lord was actually testing their faith in Him. They doubted his mentality and suddenly their future with Jesus grew dim. Unable to reconcile His words to the value of their futures, they left. Only the original twelve remained.

> *John 6:67–68 (KJV)*
> *⁶⁷ Then said Jesus unto the twelve, Will ye also go away?*
>
> *⁶⁸ Then Simon Peter answered him, Lord, to whom shall we go? thou hast the words of eternal life.*

So why did the twelve remain while the others left? They hadn't understood the Lord's words either, however, they did recognize His understanding and power over spiritual things; they had witnessed it over and over. Jesus went on to affirm their belief by simply saying that His words are spirit and eternal life.

They trusted that they would eventually understand and at the last Passover they did. The momentary confusion was not enough to make them leave. Their choice to stay and obey had been the right one.

Esther had no idea what was coming, no idea she would be called upon to save her people! She just did what she was asked to do. She obeyed! Her obedience was spiritual and beautiful!

Of His words Jesus said, "they are spirit and they are life". Obedience to God's Word is always a "Spiritual Endeavor"! We can't always see our outcomes; we just know they'll always be beautiful and life giving.

> *Esther 2:15 Now when the turn of Esther, the daughter of Abihail the uncle of Mordecai, who had taken her for his daughter, was come to go in unto the king, she required nothing but what Hegai the king's chamberlain, the keeper of the women, appointed. And Esther obtained favour in the sight of all them that looked upon her.*

It's Enough

Esther required no more help than what had been promised her. No demands made; this was never a "self" issue. It was a situation which suddenly arose in her life, one she could not have possibly anticipated.

Now the time had arrived to go in unto the king. She takes a deep breath and concludes that the provisions and preparations are enough. What had always been true about Esther will be true now. She will simply be herself.

Esther's role in God's plan was more than she knew. She only knew the things which daily appeared and yet in the end, she was more than enough.

For you, life appears the same way, moment by moment and yet like Esther the Lord has provided for you all that you need for the glorious encounter awaiting you.

Two Perspectives

While we are watching the story of Esther progress, it's important to remember that there are two perspectives present, that of the people involved and also that of God.

Indeed, life unfolds for all of us, however, while the human perspective is important to us it is not the most important one. We stand first and foremost before the eyes of God "who ordered the end from the beginning". Our destinies lie within that context, therefore, we will seek to be available and usable no matter where our lives unfold. Because God sees, we want to be seen in a favorable way. If that is true about us, we will be available, and our God will use us according to His perfect will.

That being said, we do not for one moment take for granted the value of the people for whom Jesus died. The challenge is, therefore, that the favor of God be visible in us as it was with Esther.

ELEVEN

2:16-17 (KJV)

16 So Esther was taken unto king Ahasuerus into his house royal in the tenth month, which is the month Tebeth, in the seventh year of his reign.

17 And the king loved Esther above all the women, and she obtained grace and favour in his sight more than all the virgins; so that he set he royal crown upon her head, and made her queen instead of Vashti.

Overwhelmed

If these verses do not prove that the king is overwhelmed by Esther, the rest of the account will. The fact is that Ahasuerus has never met anyone like Esther before. He seems to be transformed somehow by her. Such was her impact.

Time would prove Esther's powerful sway over the king, however, her more important sway was that upon God. This my child is a source of unspeakable joy and awe; just the way God has chosen to favor you and others like you. It is this last day army, who through the simple process of life, have found deep purpose, and have said to God, "Yes Lord, send me"! Hallelujah!

The king has fallen in love with Esther. He is, perhaps,

46

experiencing the depth of love he has never felt before. He quickly places the royal crown upon her head. His actions, both now and later, prove that Esther is far more than another Jewel in the king's collection. She has become the center of His life.

The Focal Point

Esther has become the focal point in the king's life at least while she is present with him. From this point forward, simply seeing Esther will remind the king of how much he loves her.

Isn't it amazing how Esther has gained such favor? She has been lifted into the very palace of the king and not in a staff capacity; she is there to reign right alongside the king!

To be seen as someone who occupies a very high place is not our pursuit, as warriors in this last epic battle for our families and country. Neither was it for Esther, nevertheless, still unknown to her was the absolute necessity for her to be there.

What Is That Place for Us?

Ephesians 2:4-6 (KJV)
⁴ But God, who is rich in mercy, for his great love wherewith he loved us,
⁵ Even when we were dead in sins, hath quickened us together with Christ, (by grace ye are saved;)
⁶ And hath raised us up together, and made us sit together in heavenly places in Christ Jesus:

The words in verse 6 "heavenly places" means positions above the sky. Now obviously no one reading these words is physically sitting in these heavenly places. It does, however, describe God's Divine perspective revealed in His Word, the Bible. This means for us, being raised up through salvation from a purely earthly perspective and, seeing the world through His eyes. Furthermore, it also reveals positional power given to the redeemed in order to fulfill God's Great Commission in the earth.

When we live in obedience to Biblical truth, we are favored into the most glorious and powerful place imaginable, into God's focal point. Amen

Let's remember that Esther was not the only candidate to wear the Royal Crown. There were many damsels who had also received one whole year of intense preparation in hopes of wearing it.

All had an opportunity to appear before the king and all had been received as maidens and wives unto the king. All were called, yet in the end, only one was chosen to wear the crown.

The void had been filled. Esther is Queen and so much better than Vashti!

> *Esther 2:18-20 (KJV)*
> *18 Then the king made a great feast unto all his princes and his servants, even Esther's feast; and he made a release to the provinces, and gave gifts, according to the state of the king.*
> *19 And when the virgins were gathered together the second time, then Mordecai sat in the king's gate.*
> *20 Esther had not yet shewed her kindred nor her people; as Mordecai had charged her: for Esther did the commandment of Mordecai, like as when she was brought up with him.*

The King's Celebration

A great celebration is made in honor of the crowning of Esther. In jubilant expression the king gives gifts and releases of imprisonments and indebtedness all in accordance with the king's massive wealth.

Obviously, the king is overjoyed for what has finally been accomplished. He has a new wife and queen whom he loves more than he could have expected. A social catastrophe has been averted and now the kingdom can finally return to normal.

Mordecai returns humbly to his seat as a doorkeeper in the king's court while Esther continues to love and honor him from her exalted position. Their secret concerning Esther's true ethnicity remains secure.

> ### Esther 2:21-23 (KJV)
>
> [21] In those days, while Mordecai sat in the king's gate, two of the king's chamberlains, Bigthan and Teresh, of those which kept the door, were wroth, and sought to lay hand on the king Ahasuerus.
>
> [22] And the thing was known to Mordecai, who told it unto Esther the queen; and Esther certified the king thereof in Mordecai's name.
>
> [23] And when inquisition was made of the matter, it was found out; therefore they were both hanged on a tree: and it was written in the book of the chronicles before the king.

Character

Earlier we noted that Mordecai had been advanced into a relatively significant place having been assigned a gatekeeper to the king's court. It was there that Mordecai learned directly of two extremely disgruntled co-workers who were plotting to assassinate the King. Characteristically, Mordecai does the right thing and made the matter known to Esther, in order to protect the life of the king. Again, it is not our purpose to establish virtue in king

Ahasuerus, history seems to prove the opposite (Ahasuerus marked the end of Persian favor toward Israel). Who would know the nature of Ahasuerus better than Mordecai, yet he is totally bound to his commitments and responsibilities; he is trustworthy!

We must also remember the loving care Mordecai has always provided for Esther. The planned violence declared by the two would-be assassins must not be allowed to threaten the welfare of Esther either!

Powerful Investment

Our Christ-like character, seen by God will always be a powerful deterrent to the persistent plots of the devil and his cohorts. It will shield our children and loved ones!

After an investigation is completed, the two men accused were then convicted and hanged. Because no actual attempt was made upon the king's life, the matter remained relatively quiet, however, the entire incident was officially recorded.

Impossible for Mordecai to know, was that his faithfulness would later provide "the life saving measure" which would help deliver the entire population of Jews (within the king's vast realm) from sudden death! Amen!

TWELVE

Esther 3:1 (KJV)
¹ After these things did king Ahasuerus promote Haman the son of Hammedatha the Agagite, and advanced him, and set his seat above all the princes that were with him.

Haman is considered by Israel to be the descendant of Agag the king of the Philistines. To Esther, he must have represented danger. She knew his being promoted, was not a good thing.

Remember earlier how we spoke of our work in Christ and how it is always spiritual because His word is spirit? We will do that now simply by taking a brief journey backward, even from Esther's time, in order to better understand her concern and also to further develop a necessary concern of our own.

The Double

Before we plunge any farther into chapter 3, it is imperative that we look more closely at what makes Haman "tick". The name Haman defined is "double", a synonym being "duplicate" (exact copy).

We are introduced to Haman in Esther 3:1 where he is identified as an Agagite. Remember he is a descendant of Agag!

1 Samuel 15:2 (KJV)
*² Thus saith the LORD of hosts, I remember
that which Amalek did to Israel, how he laid wait
for him in the way, when he came up from Egypt.*

These accounts took place over 450 years before Haman the Agagite was raised to power In Esther 3:1. The prophet Samuel is giving stern orders to King Saul, telling him, this mission is the most important one of his life.

Therefore, he must obey and not fail.

Then Samuel prophecies to Saul, (the Lord saying) "I remember that which Amalek did to Israel ..."

Now, let's go back 400 years more in order to see what the Lord remembered about Amalek:

(Deuteronomy 25:18-19 (KJV)
*¹⁸ How he (Amalek) met thee (Moses and the
people) by the way, and smote (kill, slaughter) the
hindmost of thee, even all that were feeble behind
thee, when thou wast faint and weary; and he feared
not God.*
*¹⁹ Therefore it shall be, when the LORD thy
God hath given thee rest from all thine enemies
round about, in the land which the LORD thy
God giveth thee for an inheritance to possess
it, that thou shalt blot out the remembrance of
Amalek from under heaven; <u>thou shalt not forget
it.</u>*

The Lord remembered the injustices wrought upon his people during a time of difficult journeying, during the Exodus. Then

God pronounces the COMPLETE ANNIHILATION OF AMALEK! Sobering.

Returning 400 years again to the prophet Samuel's time, let's listen to Samuel's commandment from God to King Saul relating to Amalek and Saul's response:

> *1 Samuel 15:3, 7-9 (KJV)*
> *³ Now go and smite Amalek, and utterly destroy all that they have, and spare them not; ...*
> *⁷ And Saul smote the Amalekites from Havilah until thou comest to Shur, that is over against Egypt.*
> *⁸ And he took Agag the king of the Amalekites alive, and utterly destroyed all the people with the edge of the sword.*
> *⁹ But Saul and the people spared Agag, and the best of the sheep, and of the oxen, and of the fatlings, and the lambs, and all that was good, and would not utterly destroy them: but everything that was vile and refuse, that they destroyed utterly.*

Finally we see historic Agag (Amalek) and his diabolical connection to Israel! Let's watch The Lord's response (along with Samuel's) to what King Saul had done.

> *1 Samuel 15:10-11 (KJV)*
> *¹⁰ Then came the word of the LORD unto Samuel, saying,*
> *¹¹ It repenteth me that I have set up Saul to be king: for he is turned back from following me, and hath not performed my commandments. And*

it grieved Samuel; and he cried unto the LORD all night.

1 Samuel 15:19-20 (KJV)
 [19] *Wherefore then didst thou not obey the voice of the LORD, but didst fly upon the spoil, and didst evil in the sight of the LORD?*
 [20] *And Saul said unto Samuel, Yea, I have obeyed the voice of the LORD, and have gone the way which the LORD sent me, and have brought Agag the king of Amalek, and have utterly destroyed the Amalekites.*

1 Samuel 15:25-26 (KJV)
 [25] *Now therefore, I pray thee, pardon my sin, and turn again with me, that I may worship the LORD.*
 [26] *And Samuel said unto Saul, I will not return with thee: for thou hast rejected the word of the LORD, and the LORD hath <u>rejected</u> thee from being king over Israel.*

1 Samuel 15:32-33 (KJV)
 [32] *Then said Samuel, Bring ye hither to me Agag the king of the Amalekites. And Agag came unto him delicately. And Agag said, Surely the bitterness of death is past.*
 [33] *And Samuel said, As thy sword hath made women childless, so shall thy mother be childless among women. <u>And Samuel hewed Agag in pieces before the LORD in Gilgal.</u>*

This is stunning! The Lord is so angry concerning Agag that He rejects Saul as king forever!

There are many things which can be taken away from this account. One of which is obvious and must be a cornerstone in our study. It is the fury which Amalek produced in the Heart of God! The Lord refused to forget, refused to walk away.

Afterward, Samuel hewed Agag in pieces (before the Lord in Gilgal)! The action Samuel took seems uncharacteristic, nevertheless, we must prepare our hearts and minds for the fearful measures the Lord will eventually take against all arrogant and ruthless men.

God will do this in America also. Let this be a sign to us all! What governments and religions fail to perform, the Prophetic Anointing will.

The Exodus Motive

Now remember, it's during the Exodus where we first saw (Deut.25:18) the terrible acts of Amalek referred to by God.

The people moaned beneath the heavy load of forced labor. Life had become miserable and deadly, for the Chosen people of God. They cried out to God and he heard them.

> *Exodus 3:7 (KJV)*
> *⁷ And the LORD said, I have surely seen the affliction of my people which are in Egypt, and have heard their cry by reason of their taskmasters; for I know their sorrows;*

The Lord's Heart

In verse 7, The Lord said, "I know their sorrows". Simply

stated, *The Lord was far more than just aware, He was deeply and personally afflicted by the suffering of His people!*

When God was finished, all of Israel was standing safely beyond the Red Sea!

In contrast, God had disgraced Egypt's every god, including Pharaoh. God had left his firstborn dead as Pharaoh had threatened Israel, and God had buried his entire army in the depths of the Red Sea!

Enter Amalek

So after centuries of bondage, painful slavery, ruthless murders, and a difficult deliverance, you can see why anger was kindled in the Heart of God. He had lately crushed Egypt, now ... Amalek?! "When he(Amalek) met thee(Moses and God's people) by the way, and smote (killed, slaughtered) the hindmost of thee, even all that were feeble behind thee, when thou wast faint and weary; and he feared not God". Deuteronomy 25:18 (KJV)

Sometimes we too wonder when the evil onslaught will end! Take heart children. Soon our battles will be over, and as more than conquerors, we will meet the Lord in the air, and so shall we ever be with the Lord!

Knowing Haman

Jesus said, "Ye are of your father, the devil, and the works of your father ye will do."

Jesus further described the devil by telling us what he always does. "He comes but to steal, kill, and destroy."

Do you see the same evil heart in Amalek? Note; "he (Amalek) ... slaughtered the feeble, the faint, and the weary and he feared not God"

Who is this exalted one? This Haman (double), son of

Hammadatha (fire)? He is none other than the "fiery double" of Agag, the heart of Satan and the Spirit of Anti-Christ.

These wicked and murderous spirits live from generation to generation and now we, like Esther, are confronted with them again. Especially that 'one' the hater of God, the instigator of all violence and murder. The 'one' who has relentlessly promoted the murder of the innocent even unto the pinnacle of slanderous slaughter, that of the unborn!

THIRTEEN

Esther 3:2 (KJV)
  ² And all the king's servants, that were in the king's gate, bowed, and reverenced Haman: for the king had so commanded concerning him. But Mordecai bowed not, nor did him reverence.

The Line Is Drawn

Once the king had advanced Haman, he also ordered that all should bow before Haman, as an extension of himself. It is important to observe that all bowed, as the king commanded, with the exception of one, that being Mordecai.

What we have learned about Agag and the Amalekites, Mordecai already knew and, along with God's people, had known for generations. When Mordecai refused to bow before Haman, he must have known there would be painful or deadly consequences. Perhaps he had hoped that they would be limited to only him.

Mordecai was bound to his Jewish faith and commitment to its laws and commandments. He would never bow to any other god or man especially an Agagite-Amalekite. He worshipped only the God of Abraham, Isaac, and Jacob. So, as often as Haman passed and all bowed before him, Mordecai did not. Eventually folks began to talk, wondering one to another, why Mordecai was allowed to ignore the king's commandment.

Esther 3:3-6 (KJV)

³ Then the king's servants, which were in the king's gate, said unto Mordecai, Why transgressest thou the king's commandment?

⁴ Now it came to pass, when they spake daily unto him, and he hearkened not unto them, that they told Haman, to see whether Mordecai's matters would stand: for he had told them that he was a Jew.

⁵ And when Haman saw that Mordecai bowed not, nor did him reverence, then was Haman full of wrath.

⁶ And he thought scorn to lay hands on Mordecai alone; for they had shewed him the people of Mordecai: wherefore Haman sought to destroy all the Jews that were throughout the whole kingdom of Ahasuerus, even the people of Mordecai.

Daily the king's servants asked and debated with Mordecai concerning his Jewish faith. This was the reason Mordecai had given for his apparent disrespect for Haman.

Eventually, the servants of the king went to Haman themselves, telling him of Mordecai's religion and how that it released Mordecai from the king's commandment, that is, to bow before him, for he is a Jew!"

It's On Now!

Having heard the report of the servants, Haman went purposefully before Mordecai and waited. He then witnessed what the servants had said was true! Mordecai did not bow nor respect him! Suddenly infuriated, Haman thought to murder Mordecai on the spot. Then, Haman reconsiders; he thinks himself too prominent to slay only one Jew, instead, "I will slaughter them all in one single day!"

> *Exodus 17:15-16 (KJV)*
> *[15] And Moses built an altar, and called the name of it Jehovahnissi:*
> *[16] For he said, Because the LORD hath sworn that <u>the LORD will have war with Amalek from generation to generation.</u>*

Suddenly, the centuries between Exodus and Esther are compressed into one moment of time. In a spiritual flash, the battle with Agag of Amalek is renewed and although, not yet revealed, it will ultimately become: Esther the Jewess vs. Haman the Agagite for the lives of God's people. Amazing!

"Destroy All The Jews!"

> *Psalm 83:1-4 (KJV)*
> *[1] Keep not thou silence, O God: hold not thy peace, and be not still, O God.*
> *[2] For, lo, thine enemies make a tumult: and they that hate thee have lifted up the head.*
> *[3] They have taken crafty counsel against thy people, and consulted against thy hidden ones.*
> *[4] They have said, Come, and let us cut them off from being a nation; <u>that the name of Israel may be no more in remembrance.</u>*

These verses refer to the historic enemies of God's people! It reveals a common hatred among them toward God and his people and their willingness to corporately plan and execute the total annihilation of them!

Remember that Haman's first inclination was to immediately kill Mordecai alone. Then a greater motivation (an ancient and spiritual one) suddenly kicked-in overriding his personal one. It's mandate; to erase God's people forever!

So instead, "Haman sought to destroy all the Jews that were throughout the whole kingdom of Ahasuerus, even the people of Mordecai." Esther 3:6 (KJV)

Here again we see, the insane arrogance and delusional thinking of the 'one' who actually believed that he could usurp the power of God, wage war and conquer Heaven! This is that ancient spirit, bent on the destruction of God's people! And, let's not kid ourselves, he totally believes that he will accomplish his desire.

A Fine Line

There is a fine line between the fantastical and the Biblical. Entertainment in our technology driven society has taken on a new dimension where everything is possible. The projections that are sold for billions and billions of dollars are only limited to the imaginations of those creating them. Fantastical concepts of creation, life, existence, and even death are daily projected. Mythical characters along with contemporary ones appear in forms we are unfamiliar with yet are made acceptable having retained just enough humanity for the audience to relate to. Superpowers allow both heroes and villains to soar far above and dragging our earth-bound imaginations with them, until the walls of the theater or of our living rooms are momentarily forgotten. The dastardliest villains ever conceptualized now do battle in the hopes of destroying our earth and its earthlings forever. Brave warriors of all shapes and fashions form the defenders of our scorched and beaten earth. Sometimes the indescribable invaders win! But not for long! Just until the next episode, you'll see!

Horror movies have become a rage also. They too are augmented by the demented minds of their creators, enabled by "cutting edge" technology.

Ruthless scabs, scavengers, and scoundrels do the devils bidding while the entertained sip our nations latest placebo, "It's only a movie."

Where do we draw the line on these types of productions? Fantasy sells, it's as simple as that! As long as they are lucrative, they will continue.

But ... what if there is some truth to what is being depicted as purely make-believe? What a stunning experience it would be, if when moviegoers exited the theater only to find the slithering and murderous creature they had just viewed awaiting them outside!

Only minutes earlier the beast was seen stomping, crushing, biting, and hurling men, women and children mercilessly through the air. A deep growling voice cursing and laughing the whole time while its human-like eyes darting back and forth seeking more powerless victims. Hopefully the multitudes would somehow get up from their place of being assaulted, bludgeoned, and bruised, but they don't, they just lay there, while new scenes continue. No attempt to make them alive again; not the unknown ones at least.

If our world wasn't really like this, it genuinely could be called fantasy but because it is, we must call it escapism instead. Especially by those doing the damage and yes also those who do nothing to prevent it, instead privately promote and encourage it.

What if there was a world like the one described, where there are ugly and gruesome creatures as fierce as they are desperate to have their way. The Bible says there is a place like that and it's near enough that if we could, we might reach out and touch it.

It is in our world! The reason we can't see it or touch it is because it is a different realm. It is where people go when they die. It is not a physical place but a spiritual one, just as real as physical, only different.

In a fantasy world, the creatures are visibly evil, loud, crushing and murderous. In our world, although invisible, they remain intensely evil. The means of warfare they employ is by tempting the multitudes into sin, which is rebellion against God! The ultimate goal is to provide world dominance for the devil himself. If effective enough, they remain concealed while the people they influence become evil, loud, crushing, and murderous themselves! Once this is accomplished in sufficient numbers, he will attempt to destroy all Jews and Christians with them! By then, the devil will have embodied a human being and will be referred to by the Saints as "The Anti-Christ."

> *Ephesians 6:10-12 (KJV)*
> *[10] Finally, my brethren, be strong in the Lord, and in the power of his might.*
> *[11] Put on the whole armour of God, that ye may be able to stand against the wiles of the devil.*
> *[12] For we wrestle not against flesh and blood, but against principalities, against powers, against the rulers of the darkness of this world, against spiritual wickedness in high places.*

In these verses, the Apostle Paul encourages us to be strong in the Lord i.e. in relationship with God and in the things which only God can provide; stating that our warfare tools must be spiritual and not physical, realizing that our enemy is a spiritual one.

Paul also reveals to us that we are combatting a spiritual army and that within its structure are levels of rank and authority. There are echelons of authority from the greatest to the smallest. The Bible likens them to dragons, serpents, scorpions, vipers, and beasts. Furthermore, they are referred to as demons, devils, (fallen) angels, and different types of spirits such as "unclean spirits and spirits of fear" and more. There is a diversity of them according to purpose, power, and appearance. Furthermore, they are massive in number.

In this book, the one opposing spirit I will focus upon, is the highest authority in this spiritual army. His desire is already well known and documented; it is world conquest including the absolute obliteration of all those who love, serve, and are owned of God. This human beast (whom we earlier identified) represents the greatest and most vicious threat God's people have ever or will ever encounter.

FOURTEEN

Esther 3:7-9 (KJV)

⁷ In the first month, that is, the month Nisan, in the twelfth year of king Ahasuerus, they cast Pur, that is, the lot, before Haman from day to day, and from month to month, to the twelfth month, that is, the month Adar.

⁸ And Haman said unto king Ahasuerus, There is a certain people scattered abroad and dispersed among the people in all the provinces of thy kingdom; and their laws are diverse from all people; neither keep they the king's laws: therefore it is not for the king's profit to suffer them.

⁹ If it please the king, let it be written that they may be destroyed: and I will pay ten thousand talents of silver to the hands of those that have the charge of the business, to bring it into the king's treasuries.

Haman

Look at Haman for a moment. Do you see what he is doing? He has ordered that Pur be cast before him. This is a form of spiritualism. He is seeking spiritual direction and power concerning the timing and the performing of his desired destruction of all Jews in Persia. He is in essence pursuing the favor of a certain ancient spirit for the success of his desire.

What spirit would he be petitioning? The one most likely to respond would obviously be the one most bent on the Jew's destruction, the greatest hater, the most jealous of them all. Haman's petition for a partner would be given ... in the form of a slithering stench of agonizing ancient arrogance. The devil himself responds in essence saying, "Now, now is the time; destroy them all!"

(Verse 9, " ... Let it be written that they may be destroyed")

> Esther 3:10-11 (KJV)
> ¹⁰ And the king took his ring from his hand, and gave it unto Haman the son of Hammedatha the Agagite, the Jews' enemy.
> ¹¹ And the king said unto Haman, The silver is given to thee, the people also, to do with them as it seemeth good to thee.

Earlier we were told that Haman had been promoted to the second highest place in the kings government. We don't know the circumstances nor the history of Haman as to why he was vaulted into such a place, only that he is Agagite.

Take My Ring!

> John 8:44 (KJV)
> ⁴⁴ Ye are of your father the devil, and the lusts of your father ye will do. He was a murderer from the beginning, and abode not in the truth, because there is no truth in him. When he speaketh a lie, he speaketh of his own: for he is a liar, and the father of it.

The Lord Jesus shows us three things which the children of the *devil always do. First, they pursue their own personal satisfaction, the evil lusts of their father. These are shared lusts, ones they have in common. What will they do to obtain them? They will lie and even murder in order to fulfill the lusts of their father.*

This is what Haman has done. Someway, he has lied, manipulated, and probably murdered in order to secure his position with Ahasuerus. It is obvious that the king is not surprised nor offended when Haman offers as a solution, the mass murder of the Jews. It would be the pinnacle of pleasure.

Do you see? For Haman and for others like him, murder is more than a necessity, it is a pleasure. It is, the satisfying of that perpetually wicked heart of their father, the devil. Listen carefully to what I am about to say. Without murder, the devil would feel less than what he believes he is. Remember, satan cares for nothing except himself. He cares nothing for Haman! He is but a vessel, a body, a tool.

Ahasuerus relates to Haman! Haman is like him, he understands him. Haman has an evil bent; they want the same things. He knows Haman will stop at nothing to get what he wants, where even murder is not an issue. They have, in essence, a brotherhood ... a father in common; the devil. "Here, take my ring ..." Then Haman and the king have drinks together.

> *Esther 3:12-15*
> *[12] Then were the king's scribes called on the thirteenth day of the first month, and there was written according to all that Haman had commanded unto the king's lieutenants, and to the governors that were over every province, and to the rulers of every people of every province according to the writing thereof, and to every people after their language; in the name of king Ahasuerus was it written, and sealed with the king's ring.*

¹³ And the letters were sent by posts into all the king's provinces, to destroy, to kill, and to cause to perish, all Jews, both young and old, little children and women, in one day, even upon the thirteenth day of the twelfth month, which is the month Adar, and to take the spoil of them for a prey.

¹⁴ The copy of the writing for a commandment to be given in every province was published unto all people, that they should be ready against that day.

¹⁵ The posts went out, being hastened by the king's commandment, and the decree was given in Shushan the palace. And the king and Haman sat down to drink; but the city Shushan was perplexed.

Haman is satisfied with the lot that was cast and begins immediately with his plan. "There is a certain people", he said. We know it was God's chosen people Israel, Haman was referring to. There is no justice in his plan! Haman is ticked off unto a monstrous proportion and now has the "ring" which is the authority to do whatever he desires against Mordecai and his people.

<u>One Year</u>

It was in the first month of the year when Haman received his green light, and the Children of God were given one year to prepare.

Beloved, it would be so very easy to go on as we always have even though we have faced or at least witnessed firsthand the signs of Christ's soon return.

The power and regularity of the signs we are seeing, make it obvious what is happening. We are in a battle, and we must not waste one moment in our effort to touch the Heart of God! Mordecai didn't and neither did Esther. Saints, we need God's rescue and we need it now.

In what form will that rescue come?

FIFTEEN

Esther 4:1–2 (KJV)
¹ When Mordecai perceived all that was done,
Mordecai rent his clothes, and put on sackcloth with
ashes, and went out into the midst of the city, and
cried with a loud and a bitter cry;
² And came even before the king's gate: for
none might enter into the king's gate clothed with
sackcloth.

<u>Resistance</u>

When Mordecai learned the details of Haman's plan and that
he had been given full authority of the king, he responded according
to the core of who he was. He rent his clothing and covered himself
with sackcloth which was apparently a disgrace and would be highly
ridiculed. Furthermore, he went out into the midst of the city where
he would likely be seen of the people. Then if that were not enough,
he cried out with a desperate and unusually mournful cry.

This was no time for pride or pretentiousness and in Mordecai
there was neither. More than any other time, what we see and hear
of Mordecai, is who he genuinely was. None of what Mordecai did
was preconceived.

This would be considered an extreme response today, even when
certain and impending dangers threaten our nearest loved ones.

Unfortunately, Mordecai's response is seldom seen in our modern "House of God". Most of the time, quiet prayers are offered up. Is it because it isn't necessary or because we don't know it yet?

Whom resist ye steadfastly in the faith.

I don't know if Mordecai had premeditated his actions and had determined that this was the beginning of a bold resistance to the mass-murderous plans of Haman and the King. Maybe not, perhaps this was the only reasonable response for the man of God, as natural a response as gasoline exposed to a flame. A fusion of fiery faith and forceful expression, frantic and focused in necessity, fearless in conclusion while calculated in God's favor. Mordecai cries out bitterly! I can't tell that this was Mordecai's plan for resistance but it couldn't help becoming one! Child of God; this could be you!

The Greek: "Αιρεται εθνος μηδεν ηδικηκος, A people are going to be destroyed, who have done no evil!"

Is there more to this? Are these desperate actions of Mordecai the "very move of God" to save the people? I believe they are, furthermore, I am convinced they are a key for us (the Church) in our desperate need for deliverance!

Remember, this was when the Children of Israel were coming out of a decades long captivity. Already there is an ongoing effort to restore the city of Jerusalem. The ultimate desire is to renew fellowship with their God, The God of Abraham, Isaac, and Jacob and what greater motive than that?

The Six Day War

This amazing and miraculous war was fought between Israel

and bordering nations: Jordan, Syria, and Egypt. It was fought between June 5 and June 10, 1967.

Normalizations between Israel and Arabs had not been established since the war they had fought in 1948 when five Arab nations invaded territory of the former Palestinian mandate shortly after Israel declared her independence. Israel had fought off the invaders and the process had gained them 21 % more territory and also diminished the validity of the Arab dominance.

It was, therefore, immensely concerning when in 1967 the Arab nations began to amass military forces on the borders of Israel, while still in her infancy of rebirth.

When Israeli military analysts had concluded that an Arab attack was imminent, it was decided to launch a pre-emptive strike against them. It seemed to be the only hope of defending the new state of Israel against this massive threat.

The Hand of God

Not long after the pre-emptive strike began, it became obvious that the Hand of God was very much involved in this effort. The war which began on June 5 was over by June 10! Israel had recaptured the entire City of Jerusalem and much more! Every indication pointed to certain defeat but instead became a mighty victory for God's people Israel.

Mordecai's Pre-emptive Strike

There are similarities between these two events in Israel's history. In both cases, Haman's threat and the joint Arab threat in 1967 seemed to be hopeless and impossible to overcome. In both, God intervened; history and a bustling nation of Israel prove it is so.

Through all of Israel's existence, their continued survival

71

has hinged upon the divine interventions of God. It has been no different with these United States of America. Although Israel is an ancient people while the United States is an infant nation of people does not diminish the peculiar and beautiful similarities and camaraderie that exists between them. In essence and not to the exclusion of all other nations, Israel was created for America and America was created for Israel.

(Numbers 24:17 (KJV) 17 I shall see him, but not now: I shall behold him, but not nigh: there shall come a Star out of Jacob, and a Sceptre shall rise out of Israel, and shall smite the corners of Moab, and destroy all the children of Sheth.) Here, Balaam prophecies of an eternal king and kingdom which would eventually rise out of Jacob (Israel).

(Isaiah 28:15-16 (KJV) 15 Because ye have said, We have made a covenant with death, and with hell are we at agreement; when the overflowing scourge shall pass through, it shall not come unto us: for we have made lies our refuge, and under falsehood have we hid ourselves:

16 Therefore thus saith the Lord GOD, Behold, I lay in Zion for a foundation a stone, a tried stone, a precious corner stone, a sure foundation: he that believeth shall not make haste.

Here, Isaiah predicts an eternal king which will secure Israel forever.

Our Star and Founding Stone

Both the "star and scepter" which Balaam predicted would rise out of Israel along with the "precious founding stone" which Isaiah predicted would rise out of Israel, were both fulfilled in the coming of our Lord Jesus Christ.

This promised King and Kingdom constitutes for the USA and Israel, "The tie that binds them together"!

We, the USA, were born and founded upon this "precious

foundation stone." Our love and allegiance was pledged to that eternal "star" King. Therefore, both our national birth, solidity, and security has come from God through Israel!

Mordecai And The USA

Was what Mordecai did then, important to us today? In other words, was the survival of Israel then, important to us now? Absolutely! The birth and success of the United States depended completely upon the birth and success of Israel. The founders of our nations have stated this unequivocally in texts.

9/11/1944

It was upon this momentous date when the first American troops stormed into Nazi Germany. Was this date (9/11) only coincidental? Would we be going out on a prophetic limb to suggest that the spirit of Hamon, Hitler, Anti-Christ was observing when the Americans arrived? Not when we consider the Marxist movement boldly displayed upon the screens of our televisions almost daily. Nope, I don't think the devil forgot ... do you?

The USA made a huge contribution in the defeat of Adolf Hitler. Furthermore, there were more Jewish refugees received into the US than any other nation.

So by the end of 1944 we began seeing the joint destinies of Israel and the USA begin to immerge upon the world scene. The United States was becoming a friend and ally of God's chosen people Israel. Hallelujah.

SIXTEEN

Pre-emptive Strike ... Praying It Forward

Was Mordecai weeping and lamenting in an effort to change Hamon's mind? Or perhaps his public display was in an effort to garner sympathy and support? Was it a desperate expression of humility even begging before the authorities of society and government? Or maybe it was a white flag of surrender and he was now willing to bow before Haman.

Weeping or Aggression?

The path of world history has been sprinkled by blood spilt at the hands of animalistic tyrants. The cries of the millions who were brutalized and murdered are recorded in heaven and there is a day of reconning coming, for that, we give God praise.

Among these many tyrants, there is one thing common among them. Their treatment of the people they considered obstacles or unnecessary to their evil plots. From their heinous fields of genocide have risen the cries of pain and suffering. To these wicked hearts, cries were simply sounds "in association" with the necessary work being accomplished. The ends justified the means. "If you want an omelet, you're going to have to crack a few eggs."

No, Haman would not be moved by the mournful weeping of Mordecai. His was no different than any other wicked heart that came before or after. In fact, it may have provided a crude satisfaction, knowing that Mordecai could not possibly stop him now.

A Precious Pastor

I remember preaching the funeral of an amazing pastor. It was a privilege for me. His commitment to God was exceptional and his work ethic was amazing. His church was small, never over fifty people and the building where they met was old and tattered.

Only a handful of the Pastor's family were involved and faithful. The majority of them were distant and uninvolved and because the Pastor was elderly and retired when he took on the work, they just didn't understand.

Pastor worked constantly to repair and improve the old building. Ultimately, because of drooping walls and settling floors, the pastor concluded that the church needed a new foundation. Originally, the church had been built directly upon the ground. After much consideration, Pastor determined that the soil beneath the church would have to be carefully dug out and the foundation poured a few feet at a time.

Pastor showed up the next day with the tools necessary to begin the work ... a shovel, a pick, and a couple of five-gallon pails. He began that morning at one corner of the church and months later had dug out the entire crawlspace one pail at a time and had poured the new foundation also one pail of concrete at a time! One other had helped part-time; he was a precious son-in-law. Pastor's amazing accomplishment had gone unapproved and unappreciated by most of his family.

During his funeral I shared a story: There was one day a small boy and his grandfather standing out in a field near the ranch-house where Grandpa lived.

They were both gazing into the sky at a majestic eagle soaring high above them. "Grandpa," the boy asked, "Why does the eagle go so high and why does he fly in a circle like that? The ducks in the pond don't do that, do they?" Then kneeling next to the boy, the Grandpa replied, "No son, the ducks don't do that and as far as the eagle goes, well my boy, I guess you'd have to be an eagle to know."

So why did Pastor do what he did? Well, I guess you'd have to be an eagle to know.

Mordecai Flying High

Mordecai's response is as bold and beautiful as the eagle rising above and overcoming the deadly storm. His loud and mournful cries would never be considered militant and yet were.

The success of a pre-emptive strike depends upon secrecy, the hidden and unexpected. The precise details and plans of the strike are only known by those who are intimately involved. The worst-case scenarios are constantly kept in mind. Those who plan the attack and those who carry it out, are one body. Each of them knew that their futures (including of their nation and family's) depended upon the success of their pre-emptive attack. Therefore, love is the primary motivation for this desperate and dangerous endeavor.

Mordecai, moved by his love for the people, love for the nation, love for their ultimate freedom, and of course, love for his daughter Esther began to cry out to the God he loved and served. Unknowingly, Mordecai's powerful public expression of love before God was the pre-emptive strike which paved the way for Israel's deliverance.

SEVENTEEN

Esther 4:3 (KJV)
³ And in every province, whithersoever the king's commandment and his decree came, there was great mourning among the Jews, and fasting, and weeping, and wailing; and many lay in sackcloth and ashes.

Romans 8:15 (KJV)
¹⁵ For ye have not received the spirit of bondage again to fear; but ye have received the Spirit of adoption, whereby we cry, Abba, Father.

<u>Linked By Love</u>

What Mordecai learned first is now known by all the Jews. They responded as he did. They mourned and cried out to God.

Now consider this, no one else was under threat of massacre; it was only the Jews. No one wept and mourned publicly while wearing sackcloth, except Mordecai, a Jew. There was only one within the Kings courts who would intervene for the Jews; it was Esther, a Jew. They all had this in common. They were Jews. They were the people of God. They were not perfect, but they were family; the ones whom God had chosen.

For us to be relevant in God's planned rescue of these United

States of America, we must be real, not just religious. God must be our Father and we must be the genuine and miraculous Children and family of God. If what the apostle Paul said is true, and indeed it is, God is our Abba; He is our Daddy!

This is our fortress, our stronghold. It will be what defines us and empowers us to fulfill God's will in this last hour. In the face of immense opposition and seeming impossibilities, our love for Christ will link us together into the greatest Christian army this world has ever seen!

Once like-minded and linked in love, we can move forward in our conquests for the Glory of God. The Bible speaks clearly of last day events and how they relate to the Church. We are equipped with that information, furthermore, "We are not ignorant of the devil's devices" i.e. we can predict what he is going to do. There will be great suffering, however, we can step <u>in</u> and weep now as a deterrent, not awaiting the inevitable! We will weep and mournfully cry out to God for those who will certainly die should our modern-day Haman succeed. Thus, we will desperately grieve and morn for the saints and for the lost ... so that they won't have to. We will win this way! Before God, we will grieve for those who will grieve, weep for those who will weep, suffer for those who will suffer, fall upon our face for those who will fall. Then, when we are finished, we will all rise together in the greatest outpourings of Jesus Christ that this modern world has seen. This is our Pre-emptive strike!

> *Esther 4:4 (KJV)*
> *⁴ So Esther's maids and her chamberlains came and told it her. Then was the queen exceedingly grieved; and she sent raiment to clothe Mordecai, and to take away his sackcloth from him: but he received it not.*

No Comfort

Having received the dark report from Mordecai, Esther is grieved and aware of the danger Mordecai is in. Assuming Mordecai would be comforted knowing that the queen was now attentive to the emergency, she sent raiment to Mordecai in hopes he would remove his sackcloth. Mordecai, however, refused to trade his sackcloth for the raiment. There would be no turning back, no pretending that things were less perilous than first perceived. No, the sackcloth would remain until he and Esther were one in pain and purpose.

We too have been alerted to the plans forged against our great nation and the foundations upon which she is built. We will not be relieved of our burden. We will continue in our peculiar pain until we and our God are one in purpose and power. We will not be pacified no matter who becomes aware of our plight. We know the answer lies within the circle of the Saints. Central to this great effort will be that great "Sister" movement, which like Esther, God has meticulously and powerfully raised up "for such a time as this". Glory!

> **Esther 4:5 (KJV)**
> [5] *Then called Esther for Hatach, one of the king's chamberlains, whom he had appointed to attend upon her, and gave him a commandment to Mordecai, to know what it was, and why it was.*

Hatach

Because of the confinement placed upon the wives of the king, Esther could not speak directly to Mordecai. Instead she sent Hatach who would be her messenger. She obviously trusted him. Hatach was probably a eunuch and an officer.

Beloved, as our circle tightens around the Lord Christ, it is *so important that we know the people there. We must be able to trust one another no matter what might happen. That may seem extreme, however, even the prayers we pray will be an issue and held under scrutiny by the enemies of our soul. The plans and revelations we receive from God's Spirit will have to be held and closely guarded. `*

> ### Esther 4:5-17 (KJV)
>
> ⁵ *Then called Esther for Hatach, one of the king's chamberlains, whom he had appointed to attend upon her, and gave him a commandment to Mordecai, to know what it was, and why it was.*
>
> ⁶ *So Hatach went forth to Mordecai unto the street of the city, which was before the king's gate.*
>
> ⁷ *And Mordecai told him of all that had happened unto him, and of the sum of the money that Haman had promised to pay to the king's treasuries for the Jews, to destroy them.*
>
> ⁸ *Also he gave him the copy of the writing of the decree that was given at Shushan to destroy them, to shew it unto Esther, and to declare it unto her, and to charge her that she should go in unto the king, to make supplication unto him, and to make request before him for her people.*
>
> ⁹ *And Hatach came and told Esther the words of Mordecai.*
>
> ¹⁰ *Again Esther spake unto Hatach, and gave him commandment unto Mordecai;*
>
> ¹¹ *All the king's servants, and the people of the king's provinces, do know, that whosoever, whether man or woman, shall come unto the king into the inner court, who is not called, there is one law of*

his to put him to death, except such to whom the king shall hold out the golden sceptre, that he may live: but I have not been called to come in unto the king these thirty days.

¹² And they told to Mordecai Esther's words.

¹³ Then Mordecai commanded to answer Esther, Think not with thyself that thou shalt escape in the king's house, more than all the Jews.

¹⁴ For if thou altogether holdest thy peace at this time, then shall their enlargement and deliverance arise to the Jews from another place; but thou and thy father's house shall be destroyed: and who knoweth whether thou art come to the kingdom for such a time as this?

¹⁵ Then Esther bade them return Mordecai this answer,

¹⁶ Go, gather together all the Jews that are present in Shushan, and fast ye for me, and neither eat nor drink three days, night or day: I also and my maidens will fast likewise; and so will I go in unto the king, which is not according to the law: and if I perish, I perish.

¹⁷ So Mordecai went his way, and did according to all that Esther had commanded him.

A Life-saving Plan

Here we see a conversation had between Mordecai and Queen Esther and not just any conversation. The lives and futures of many of God's people lie in the balance. The first variable in its effectiveness is its "go-between" Hatach.

It required his loyalty and his accuracy in receiving the message and also its delivery.

Our Involvement

Look at how deeply entrenched Mordecai and Esther are in the dire situation which had suddenly enveloped them. It became apparent that within a few months an evil atmosphere had been created and within that atmosphere a deadly plot, already in motion.

Let's pause for a moment and again consider the desperate circumstances which have suddenly descended upon our own nation and people. It has been at times almost overwhelming. We, as the Children of God, are seeing it as the last great effort of the enemy to destroy God's jewel and living witness in the world, the Church, more specifically to us, the American Church. Which has been a lighthouse to the entire world.

Our involvement is not an option. We are the target, just as God's people were to Haman. The only choice we have, is how we will engage this imminent threat together.

The character of our involvement is found within the hearts and lives of Mordecai and Esther. First, Mordecai was a lightning rod. In other words, he was an obvious target; he refused to bow to Haman once Haman had been advanced to that place of authority. Mordecai was faithful in every aspect of service to God. His allegiance was to God alone. Therefore, the tip of the spear in God's great push-back will be "The Faithful". Indeed, The visibly faithful!

EIGHTEEN

Esther 5:1-2 (KJV)

¹ Now it came to pass on the third day, that Esther put on her royal apparel, and stood in the inner court of the king's house, over against the king's house: and the king sat upon his royal throne in the royal house, over against the gate of the house.

² And it was so, when the king saw Esther the queen standing in the court, that she obtained favour in his sight: and the king held out to Esther the golden sceptre that was in his hand. So Esther drew near, and touched the top of the sceptre.

The Third Day

Esther's third day scenario is such a beautiful standard, not just one of excellence, but one of glorious and victorious warfare. The very thought of it draws us back to the empty tomb of Jesus our Lord and Saviour. This is the place where I endeavor to begin everyday. What a miraculous feeling arises within me when I consider the life I received there.

Esther knows what is at stake and also what is required. Haman's plan has been fully laid-out before her and the thought of Hamon being successful is staggering.

Unfortunately, the severity of our season continues to allude most citizens. Those who pursue the demise of the American church have launched an attack which is dark, dastardly, wretched, and more murderous than we dare to imagine and yet there is little desperation. Let me explain why. The overall conscience of the people has been extensively desensitized. The Bible refers to it as "having their conscience seared with a hot iron." The road to our hardness and blindness has been paved with the blood of the innocent. Having known the horrors of abortion for nearly two generation with no national uprising against it has caused our nation to accept it as a normal and necessary social practice. This legitimized, and legalized national crime has reduced our ability to fear any consequences, retributions, or judgements from God or man. Therefore, from the peoples twisted perspective, everything is ok, no matter how bad it gets. As a result, our people are grossly unprepared for what is already happening.

Esther is fully informed! Having clothed herself in royal apparel, she is prepared to approach King Ahasuerus. She and the people have been fasting and praying for her success. Should the king reject her approach, she will be executed. Nevertheless, she is willing for the sake of her people.

Risk

Luke 18:1-8 (KJV)
¹ And he spake a parable unto them to this end, that men ought always to pray, and not to faint;
² Saying, There was in a city a judge, which feared not God, neither regarded man:
³ And there was a widow in that city; and she came unto him, saying, Avenge me of mine adversary.

⁴ And he would not for a while: but afterward he said within himself, Though I fear not God, nor regard man;

⁵ Yet because this widow troubleth me, I will avenge her, lest by her continual coming she weary me.

⁶ And the Lord said, Hear what the unjust judge saith.

⁷ And shall not God avenge his own elect, which cry day and night unto him, though he bear long with them?

<u>*⁸ I tell you that he will avenge them speedily. Nevertheless when the Son of man cometh, shall he find faith on the earth?*</u>

What is the thing, which characterizes the 'kind of faith,' The Lord Jesus is showing us in this portion of scripture? Here is a woman whom the Bible refers to as a widow. She has experienced a painful crime perpetrated somehow upon herself, family, or perhaps properties.

She obviously does not have the advocacy of a husband nor is any other mentioned. She goes to the judge alone and pleads her case before him. Remember, he is an unjust judge.

<u>Injustice</u>

Here is where we begin to relate to the plight of the widow. Never in the brief history of our great nation have we seen such gross and unopposed injustice. It seems to have gained a free reign in our society, until the righteousness of God is not even a consideration within most official leadership. Rulings or actions among authorities, including judges, are based largely upon personal opinion or agenda i.e. what is right according to what they as a whole have determined. Having already dismissed Bible

85

Truth as useless and irrelevant, it is not a consideration during the decision process.

This seems to be the attitude of the unjust judge to whom Jesus is referring. However, his apparent rejection of the evidence provided, does not hinder her determination. It may all seem unworthy of official attention to the unjust judge, it is not to this very determined widow.

Motivation

What motivates this woman? It is the pain of personal injustice! It burned in her heart like a fire until her personal welfare was no longer priority. The only thing that can quench this flame is either to see justice served or to die trying! What is the faith in that, you ask? It is knowing that this unjust judge has the power to make things right. "If I can somehow, someway convince him to do so". And that is exactly what she did! She convinced him and not upon the merits of her case but rather for the fact that she simply would not give up! Her passionate pursuit of justice brought the victory. And what of her adversaries? JUSTICE WAS DONE!

Remnant Faith

This ordinary woman became extraordinary under the most difficult of circumstances. Once again let me remind you of the central purpose of this book. It is to proclaim that God is raising up an army of Godly women who will display the same passion for justice.

The unjust judge ultimately relented to a determination greater than his own. Her faith was characterized as the type of faith the Lord Jesus will seek at his return, a time of great peril and persecution. Now, we are seeing these Biblical prophecies forming before our very eyes!

As these difficult times intensify, many will compromise and eventually surrender. This, the Lord will allow as a testing and purifying process in order to form a remnant. It is within the heart of these remaining, where we find that peculiar and wonderful faith. The faith that seems to flourish in the fires of opposition. It is that faith which assumes risk as a necessary path to victory; then runs as hard and fast as it can.

Romans 13:14 (KJV)
¹⁴ But put ye on the Lord Jesus Christ, and make not provision for the flesh, to fulfil the lusts thereof.

<u>Royal Apparel</u>

Remember it is upon this "third day" that Esther has clothed herself in royal apparel. Esther has a plan and as she enters the courts of the King, she is prepared. Esther is there because of her willingness to do what it takes in order to save her people. She is aware of the dangers that exist.

The apparel she wore represented the approval she had gained. She had always been obedient and honorable. Now she returns to the king who clothed her but with a new awareness. Lives depend upon a favorable response from the king.

This is the essence of life saving intercession! It is discovering the favor which became yours when your King robed you in the first place. It is no accident that your heart is broken for a sin ravaged world, where the most innocent suffer needlessly. No! It is what you were called to be from the very foundations of the earth. Just as Esther was, " ...for such a time as this". Listen, don't despair for a lack of access to a dying world but rather rejoice in the fact that you are highly approved and that you have complete access to Jesus. It is He who clothed you in royal apparel and will receive you day or night. Then, in earnest, will desire to hear your prayers. Amen.

Esther 5:2

And it was so, when the king saw Esther the queen standing in the court, that she obtained favour in his sight: and the king held out to Esther the golden sceptre that was in his hand. So Esther drew near, and touched the top of the sceptre

A Dreadful Law

There is historical account which indicates that Esther was profoundly moved, stricken with faintness upon the turning and looking of the king. Appearing furious for the unexpected entry, it is believed that Esther received physical support from two maidens who had accompanied her.

Fighting to maintain her composure while bearing upon her heart the welfare of her people, Queen Esther teeters as though she would fall.

How beautiful and vulnerable are those who have embraced the Heart of Christ. They are apt to spend themselves all together for the sake of those for whom Jesus died. They weep from a place only God could have birthed in them. Esther's love has invested her to such a degree that it seems to Ahasuerus as though she is perishing for it. Stricken with fear and touched by God, the king rushed to Esther, embraced her, until she came again to herself. She was immediately delivered from that dreadful law which could have executed her and left her people hopeless. Instead, embraced by the king, she is now positioned to conquer her enemy and to save her people. Glory.

Esther 5:3–6 (KJV)
³ Then said the king unto her, What wilt thou, queen Esther? and what is thy request? it shall be even given thee to the half of the kingdom.

⁴ And Esther answered, If it seem good unto the king, let the king and Haman come this day unto the banquet that I have prepared for him.

⁵ Then the king said, Cause Haman to make haste, that he may do as Esther hath said. So the king and Haman came to the banquet that Esther had prepared.

⁶ And the king said unto Esther at the banquet of wine, What is thy petition? and it shall be granted thee: and what is thy request? even to the half of the kingdom it shall be performed.

Patients for Promise

Jesus said that we must, "love our enemies". If we were to hate our enemies it would directly set us against them, placing us between them and Jesus. Whereas loving them removes our negative motive and gives our Lord free access in order to fulfill His will in them. Esther had never heard the voice of Jesus but responded as though she had. She was put in an advocate's position between the enemy and her people. Instinctively, she expressed hospitality toward Haman contrary to what she really felt in order to give way for God's will in Haman's life.

We are given immeasurable promise in God's Word and we desperately need them now. Symbolically, we are seeing gallows being constructed before our very eyes in these United States of America. Strategic and malicious steps are being made against those who adhere to the Bible and hold it as being the chief cornerstone in our national foundation. Step by step they work methodically building their gallows of hatred in hopes of destroying all faith in the Bible and especially those who refuse to bow to their dark power and authority.

While Haman was focused upon Mordecai, his greater

threat was being embraced by the king himself and was given a promise greater than Haman could have ever expected ..." unto half of my kingdom". The villains of this story were not threatened by Esther which is also true of our time and situation. Nevertheless, this modern-day Esther movement is the greatest threat of all.

It comes in a time when the role of women in society-building via the nuclear family is being attacked at every level. In the midst, however, is a quiet place, where this body of women is being tightly embraced by God himself and where the still small voice of The Lord can be heard saying, "If ye shall ask anything in my name, I will do it."

My Wife

I have experienced abundant blessing through the "favor of God" which rests upon my wife Cordalee. Not just small issues of importance either. God has anointed her to bring life-saving miracles in many different forms. Her integrity is stellar, in fact, there is no prophetic voice in the earth I would trust more than my wife's. Of a truth, an army of women like my wife would turn this world upside down and I assure you, it wouldn't take long!

This Esther movement must be recognized, appreciated, and prayed for. No group has been hurt more by this ruthless and callous thrust than women especially mothers and their children. Every effort has been made to drive mothers and their children apart hoping to alienate them from each other forever. The pain of these effected mothers who were once alienated daughters, God is going to use in a mighty and magnificent way. Perhaps you were one of the alienated ones. Having always struggled to feel valuable and appreciated in more than a superficial way.

Second Fiddle

Now, however, millions of you have discovered true self-worth in Christ Jesus. You have found His love and redeeming power and in it, have become a Child of God. In His embrace, you know you will never feel second fiddle to anyone or anything ever again!

Esther had no mother, but she did have a great father through adoption and now so do you! Like Esther then, your miracle is just beginning now. The One who is able to do "exceedingly abundantly more than you can ask or think" is asking you to ask Him for more than you can imagine. You see, He loves you immeasurably; He longs to give you the desires of your heart. A world on the brink of destruction needs someone with your position and influence with God Almighty. Don't think twice about how God will respond to your approach. He will respond in no lesser way than Ahasuerus did to Esther.

> *Esther 5:7-8 (KJV)*
> *⁷ Then answered Esther, and said, My petition and my request is;*
> *⁸ If I have found favour in the sight of the king, and if it please the king to grant my petition, and to perform my request, let the king and Haman come to the banquet that I shall prepare for them, and I will do to morrow as the king hath said.*

One More Day

We don't know why Esther desired one more day before revealing her request to the king. Howbeit, her desire did not allow for conspiracy or suspicion but rather with the joy of banqueting and light conversation.

No wonder Jesus exhorts us to love our enemies. I seriously doubt that Esther held any contempt or hatred, even toward Haman. Her second banquet would be no less beautiful and bountiful than the first. Haman's return to the table was essential and although a suspicious man, he seems oblivious to Esther's design. Don't misunderstand beloved; I do not believe Esther desired the destruction of Haman but the deliverance of her people. This too will be the nature of this great Esther-like movement in America. It will in no wise be hateful, nevertheless, sufficiently powerful to move the Heart of our King Jesus! Our victory will come at a banqueting table, rich with vessels overflowing with prayer and praise. While platters irresistibly heated by deep repentance are placed before the King. Love and efficiency will make this gentle army useable to God in this critical moment in our history.

Generous Genius

Luke 6:38 (KJV)
[38] Give, and it shall be given unto you; good measure, pressed down, and shaken together, and running over, shall men give into your bosom. For with the same measure that ye mete withal it shall be measured to you again.

The generosity of our hands will make the fruit of our lips more acceptable even delectable to the Heart of God when we pray. Ahasuerus was actually anxious to give to Esther and let me remind you, he was willing to give her half of his KINGDOM! Perhaps we, like Esther, should spend more time in preparations to give rather than to receive. Hers was generous genius.

We are learning to give generously. It is a small thing to greatly give in order to see the lives of our family members saved. Esther had been praying, fasting, and waiting upon the Lord for *a massive deliverance and what better way to do that than with deeds of generosity?*

Intercessor

It was obvious what Esther's life had become. She would fast for the people; it may have seemed like something else, but in the end, it was all about the people. She loved them and embraced the opportunity she was given to save them; she knew it was from God. She became an intercessor and enlisted Mordecai and all the people to do likewise.

This last great move of God here in America and around the world will embody brave and Godly women who love their families, but not only them, they will love all people and will gladly become intercessors for them.

> ### Esther 6:1-3 (KJV)
>
> ¹ On that night could not the king sleep, and he commanded to bring the book of records of the chronicles; and they were read before the king.
>
> ² And it was found written, that Mordecai had told of Bigthana and Teresh, two of the king's chamberlains, the keepers of the door, who sought to lay hand on the king Ahasuerus.
>
> ³ And the king said, What honour and dignity hath been done to Mordecai for this? Then said the king's servants that ministered unto him, There is nothing done for him.

On That Night

... And what a critical night it was. The quiet time for sleep had arrived and yet, how could the king possibly sleep having just experienced such a momentous evening with the wife of his heart ... Esther. Perpetually bound in his mind how he might

enlarge the borders of his kingdom, now, finds himself unable to grasp this immeasurable love he feels. So overwhelmed by it, blurts out, "unto half of my kingdom!" And for a moment becomes the boy he once was, unaccustomed to the pursuits of an adult but rather found running across a field in pursuit of a butterfly. He cannot sleep. Then sighing deeply, calls for the book of records, the meat and measure of his kingdom. Then, not knowing where to begin, thrust his finger into the accrued account and by the providence of God, opened it upon the time when Mordecai had saved his life.

Saved

Oh my beloved, how many times have we unknowingly been saved by God?

I am deeply moved by the times I am aware of. How much more if suddenly I became aware of every time He has? I suppose I would soar to higher heights of praise and adoration. I would bow at His feet longer then rise and shout His glory louder.

I am convinced, my fears would be less knowing what he has done for me while I was yet afraid and doubting. How tiny my faith has been in comparison to His goodness and unfathomable love. So much better I would be now, had I spent all those sleepless nights in worship and praise, rather than in the wringing of hands in fear, of what might transpire tomorrow. He loves us! We may rest in that. Amen.

Friends

And what of our friends and family who have so faithfully served God? People, we and others have taken for granted. What a difference they have made in the lives of so many. Faithfulness and integrity, mostly done in secret; these things cannot be taken for granted and in Mordecai's case were not; God was watching.

Luke 7:34 (KJV)

³⁴ The Son of man is come eating and drinking; and ye say, Behold a gluttonous man, and a winebibber, a friend of publicans and sinners!

It was the account of what Mordecai had done mostly in secret which, when read by the king, made him an instant friend and national treasure. Can you imagine the surprise? "What honor and dignity hath been done to Mordecai?"

I too was set upon a course, one I knew pretty well, learning to love as a man what I had hated as a boy, the hard work of a farmer. I was the 'third generation farmer', and there was much at stake.

It was during the deep recession of the 1980s when prices were low and the cost of production high. The soil was grinding my young spirit to powder. I could hardly cope. When in a small country church during a special service, I made a discovery not unlike king Ahasuerus. Off the page arose the news of what a very special man had done for me. It changed my life forever.

At that point, all I could think about was, what I might do for Jesus! A lifetime later and nothing has changed. Blessed Christ forever. I Love you.

Payday

I have learned and have shared these words with many aspiring servants of God, "The Lord doesn't always pay on Friday but there is a payday coming; He has never failed me."

NINETEEN

Esther 6:4-6 (KJV)

⁴ And the king said, Who is in the court? Now Haman was come into the outward court of the king's house, to speak unto the king to hang Mordecai on the gallows that he had prepared for him.

⁵ And the king's servants said unto him, Behold, Haman standeth in the court. And the king said, Let him come in.

⁶ So Haman came in. And the king said unto him, What shall be done unto the man whom the king delighteth to honour? Now Haman thought in his heart, To whom would the king delight to do honour more than to myself?

Divine Intervention

What we see unfolding in the Word of God is His intervention. The Lord is ordering the outcome of this terrifying season in the lives of His people. We read and rejoice in the past tense; however, Esther and the people were still praying in fear and trembling. They knew only the intentions of wicked Haman. His was an inexplicable evil and at a time when things seemed to be getting better. Who is this man? What drives him unto such evil? What *have we done that would merit such an overwhelming hatred? We have discussed this very thing in an earlier chapter.*

Familiar Feelings

If you haven't felt these same sentiments, you will soon. God's people have once again become the target of wicked men, some more powerful than others, some more ruthless than others. Their motives may vary but the force that unites and drives them is the same. Theirs was Satan in Haman. Ours is also Satan in Anti-Christ (soon to be revealed). Sound impossible? The deniability of all this is still possible but only to those who would live in denial while clinging to this dying world. The good news is, that God's merciful intervention will become more and more evident as time goes by. Remember, Haman believes he has won. We know better. Hallelujah. In this current and epic battle of our own, we also know who wins. Jesus wins and we win in Him; the Bible tells us so!

Early

Impatient Haman arrives at the king's court early. Haman is twisted and debauched. Frankly speaking, he wants Mordecai dead. Now! Having received such favor lately, it doesn't seem unreasonable that the king would grant him license to kill Mordecai now. What difference would it make, they would all die soon anyway.

Who can possibly probe the depths of such a wicked and hopeless heart, and yet, this is the very essence of what we are encountering now. I grieve when I consider the pain that has been inflicted, just in my lifetime. It is an inescapable reality. If men are not to cry ... I am no man for I do daily. My heart longs to weep for the hurting, then, it leaps to find Jesus in the midst of their pain! It is a deep furrow we plow when we pray for the broken.

Instead of making his way to the king, the king met him

halfway! Why was the king so early in his court? Before Haman could inquire, the king began to speak. "What shall be done unto the man whom the king delighteth to honor?

Now, consider for a moment, the psychotic nature of Haman. The Persian kingdom is vast and deep yet within a moment, Haman concludes that the king is talking about him. The king loves him most.

What A Difference A Day Makes

How often my spirit groans within me when I consider the depths to which our great nation has sunk. My heart weeps for the grim realities that suddenly rush over me. The value of lives we have mercilessly discarded can only be measured by the sacrifice made on the Cross of Calvary. "For God So Loved The World ..." doesn't that also apply to the tiniest, the most vulnerable, to the most taken for granted? A million times yes! That is exactly why our God is raising up a standard! Unlike the devil's flood of murder, this is so much greater! A flood of hope, of sensitivity, of nurturing, of power, of rescue, of life and salvation! God's darling army! "for such a time as this" ... American Esther!

Defeated by a woman?! The concept would have been laughable to Haman. Not so much when he began to make his ascent upon the gallows, the same gallows he had constructed for Mordecai. Oh yes, read on in your bible; the victory is won.

Likewise, those who would laugh now, will not be laughing in the near future. What a difference a day has made in the Esther account. Beloved our day is coming also. Don't despair just pray. Jesus is waiting for you there.

Esther 6:7-11 (KJV)
⁷ And Haman answered the king, For the man whom the king delighteth to honour,

⁸ Let the royal apparel be brought which the king useth to wear, and the horse that the king rideth upon, and the crown royal which is set upon his head:

⁹ And let this apparel and horse be delivered to the hand of one of the king's most noble princes, that they may array the man withal whom the king delighteth to honour, and bring him on horseback through the street of the city, and proclaim before him, Thus shall it be done to the man whom the king delighteth to honour.

¹⁰ Then the king said to Haman, Make haste, and take the apparel and the horse, as thou hast said, and do even so to Mordecai the Jew, that sitteth at the king's gate: let nothing fail of all that thou hast spoken.

¹¹ Then took Haman the apparel and the horse, and arrayed Mordecai, and brought him on horseback through the street of the city, and proclaimed before him, Thus shall it be done unto the man whom the king delighteth to honour.

Never Enough

Here we see both the inflated attitude and aspiration of Haman. As he would have clothed himself, he has now clothed Mordecai. That same morning came Haman to the king hoping to kill Mordecai but instead is ordered to honor him as he would himself. And from the king's perspective, honor could never be enough. Mordecai had saved his life. Therefore, what would have been unreasonable for Haman is suitable for 'Mordecai the faithful', the man of God.

Galatians 6:9 "And let us not be weary in well doing: for in due season we shall reap, if we faint not". Child don't be discouraged, soon God will bless you beyond measure! Hallelujah!

Esther 6:12–14 (KJV)

¹² And Mordecai came again to the king's gate. But Haman hasted to his house mourning, and having his head covered.

¹³ And Haman told Zeresh his wife and all his friends every thing that had befallen him. Then said his wise men and Zeresh his wife unto him, If Mordecai be of the seed of the Jews, before whom thou hast begun to fall, thou shalt not prevail against him, but shalt surely fall before him.

¹⁴ And while they were yet talking with him, came the king's chamberlains, and hasted to bring Haman unto the banquet that Esther had prepared.

Only Human

We are the same my beloved. It is intimidating and, at times, foreboding to see the enemies of God's people. We see them in a position of great power, able to wield it at any moment. Furthermore, they have gone as far as to say that they will, if necessary!

Still, carefully look at Haman at this critical moment. He returns to his home weeping, groveling, grieving. This seems out of character for Haman to do so. Howbeit, He has encountered the Living God, the God of Mordecai, Esther, and our God.

Haman is after all human, just as those who have arrayed themselves against us. As Haman fell, so will these fall and great will be our victory, our revival!

Bad News

In despair, Haman told his wife and wise men what had befallen him on that day. "If Mordecai be of the seed of the Jews ... thou shalt surely fall"

100

Beloved we must maintain our perspective! Jesus must remain the central figure in our lives. What was bad news for Haman was good news for God's people and it didn't happen without effort. We will persevere!

Somehow, Haman's wife and counselors knew that there was favor among the Jews and that the rule of Persia over them was fragile at best. "If Mordecai be of the seed of the Jews ... thou shalt surely fall."

> *Romans 3:29 (KJV)*
> *²⁹ Is he the God of the Jews only? is he not also of the Gentiles? Yes, of the Gentiles also:*

Our Glory

The power of Mordecai's victory was the power of that covenant and it was great, however, the power of ours is greater for it not of the blood of animals but of the very Blood of Jesus Christ our Saviour. It is our Glory also!

> *"Romans 8:27-28 (KJV)*
> *²⁷ And he that searcheth the hearts knoweth what is the mind of the Spirit, because he maketh intercession for the saints according to the will of God.*
> *²⁸ And we know that all things work together for good to them that love God, to them who are the called according to his purpose.".*

What Haman thought was his day, was Mordecai's after all. Now what the enemy sees as a glimmer of success will soon become the greatest revival these United States of America have ever experienced; Pray Esther Pray!

Esther 6:14, 7:1-6

¹⁴ And while they were yet talking with him, came the king's chamberlains, and hasted to bring Haman unto the banquet that Esther had prepared.

¹ So the king and Haman came to banquet with Esther the queen.

² And the king said again unto Esther on the second day at the banquet of wine, What is thy petition, queen Esther? and it shall be granted thee: and what is thy request? and it shall be performed, even to the half of the kingdom.

³ Then Esther the queen answered and said, If I have found favour in thy sight, O king, and if it please the king, let my life be given me at my petition, and my people at my request:

⁴ For we are sold, I and my people, to be destroyed, to be slain, and to perish. But if we had been sold for bondmen and bondwomen, I had held my tongue, although the enemy could not countervail the king's damage.

⁵ Then the king Ahasuerus answered and said unto Esther the queen, Who is he, and where is he, that durst presume in his heart to do so?

⁶ And Esther said, The adversary and enemy is this wicked Haman. Then Haman was afraid before the king and the queen.

One can only wonder what was going through Haman's mind at this point. (Let's speculate) Could it be possible that Mordecai has been raised above even himself, and if so, could Mordecai overthrow his evil plans, and depending upon how much favor is given to Mordecai, would the king simply change his edict toward the Jews or would it be sufficient to vilify him also?

Obviously I don't know what he was thinking, however, one thing I do know is this; Haman cares for no one save himself and now, he is afraid.

This is that murderous spirit of darkness, the devil, in Haman. It aspires unto great evil and overthrow. In our age it is anti-Christ which aspires to the same, however now, its purpose is to destroy all faith and hope in Jesus, from our youngest Americans unto our oldest, until all that is left is fear unto despair. Still, and let me remind you, these that move against Jesus are only human and, as human saints, we will do what we are called to do, and that is to pray and obey. The spiritual part, the Lord will take care of Himself. Amen! One more thing: The enemy of our souls is afraid and justifiably so, for God is raising up an army of Esther's and we give Him praise for it.

What Is Thy Petition?

Reunited in the parlor of banquet, we find the King, Haman, and Esther while Mordecai and the people pray from a distance. Note, nothing brings the presence and wonder of God more than when we agree to bear a burden for those whom Jesus died for upon the cross. When we become consistent in this, we will certainly hear the Lord say to us, "What is thy Petition?"

Esther replies: "If I have found favour in thy sight oh King ..." Now it becomes clear what Esther's purpose has been. It has been faithfulness unto favour, to be as beautiful as she could possibly be in every aspect of her life, to God first and then to rain it down upon all others. No hate nor avarice in any of this, only love and Godly respect.

Remember, the king was also compliant in the plot to destroy the Jews, however, the faithfulness of Mordecai and Esther is *sufficient to unravel every plan of the devil in favor of them and God's people.*

No matter how great the opposition we encounter in this last day, our God is greater still and in Him, we ... will ... overcome!

We Are Sold To Perish

Myself and all my people will die if this person should succeed! How many people did or could have cried these very words throughout history. Many along the way; I think of the Jews, the holocaust of World War 2. It was a horror beyond human comprehension. Who, what kind of man could determine to do such a thing? Could this have occurred to Ahasuerus once the details of Haman's plan were revealed?

These are the realms of the unthinkable, and although unthinkable; they are now also undeniable. Whereas Adolph Hitler murdered six million of God's chosen, we have murder 70 million of God's innocent.

A Monument For Grieving

A privilege these two treasured peoples have been denied was a personal burial place. A focal point for grieving. Today we remember them as never before while the fringes of evil slither closer and closer, and we will do so with faith and fervent fire! Until it becomes impossible for that spirit of anti-Christ to advance his efforts. We will remain a blockade until we be taken out of the way (2Thes. 2)! It is here. It is now. We will have revival come hell or high water! Let truth be discovered and let Christ be Glorified!

Esther 7:7-10 (KJV)
⁷ And the king arising from the banquet of wine in his wrath went into the palace garden: and Haman stood up to make request for his life to Esther the

queen; for he saw that there was evil determined against him by the king.

⁸ Then the king returned out of the palace garden into the place of the banquet of wine; and Haman was fallen upon the bed whereon Esther was. Then said the king, Will he force the queen also before me in the house? As the word went out of the king's mouth, they covered Haman's face.

⁹ And Harbonah, one of the chamberlains, said before the king, Behold also, the gallows fifty cubits high, which Haman had made for Mordecai, who had spoken good for the king, standeth in the house of Haman. Then the king said, Hang him thereon.

¹⁰ So they hanged Haman on the gallows that he had prepared for Mordecai. Then was the king's wrath pacified.

Truth

What a powerful thing it is when finally undiscovered truths are revealed, especially when the lives of the people are weighed in the balance. The scales of God's righteousness will always tip in favor of those who hold to the truth no matter the cost. He will vindicate them. He will rescue them. He always has and He always will. Jesus said," I am the way, the truth, and the life." Our pursuit of the Truth is everything to us and yet it is (for our unspeakable benefit) personified in our marvelous and wonderous Savior Jesus Christ. The truth we cherish and honor is not abstract, it is as understandable as the death of our Lord on the cross of Calvary. We embrace the truth that first embraced us!

ABOUT THE AUTHOR

DANIEL RUBALCABA is a veteran of ministry, ten years as pastor and twenty five years as intenerate evangelist. Born, raised, and ultimately a farmer himself, Daniel has a unique perspective on Biblical teaching you will appreciate. He has witnessed many salvations in his meetings. Miracles of physical healing are also numerous and amazing. Daniel himself has been the recipient of amazing miracles to numerous to mention here.

Printed in the United States
by Baker & Taylor Publisher Services